Tax Treaty Interpretation in Light of the Vienna Convention on the Law of Treaties

Tax Treaty Interpretation in Light of the Vienna Convention on the Law of Treaties

Edited by

Georg Kofler

Michael Lang

Pasquale Pistone

Alexander Rust

Josef Schuch

Karoline Spies

Claus Staringer

Rita Szudoczky

Wolters Kluwer

Published by:
Kluwer Law International B.V.
PO Box 316
2400 AH Alphen aan den Rijn
The Netherlands
E-mail: lrs-sales@wolterskluwer.com
Website: www.wolterskluwer.com/en/solutions/kluwerlawinternational

Sold and distributed by:
Wolters Kluwer Legal & Regulatory U.S.
920 Links Avenue
Landisville, PA 17538
United States of America
E-mail: customer.service@wolterskluwer.com

ISBN 978-94-035-4488-5

e-Book: ISBN 978-94-035-4498-4
web-PDF: ISBN 978-94-035-4508-0

Tax Treaty Interpretation in Light of the Vienna Convention on the Law of Treaties

Edited by

Georg Kofler
Michael Lang
Pasquale Pistone
Alexander Rust
Josef Schuch
Karoline Spies
Claus Staringer
Rita Szudoczky

Wolters Kluwer

Published by:
Kluwer Law International B.V.
PO Box 316
2400 AH Alphen aan den Rijn
The Netherlands
E-mail: lrs-sales@wolterskluwer.com
Website: www.wolterskluwer.com/en/solutions/kluwerlawinternational

Sold and distributed by:
Wolters Kluwer Legal & Regulatory U.S.
920 Links Avenue
Landisville, PA 17538
United States of America
E-mail: customer.service@wolterskluwer.com

ISBN 978-94-035-4488-5

e-Book: ISBN 978-94-035-4498-4
web-PDF: ISBN 978-94-035-4508-0

Editors

Prof. DDr **Georg Kofler** has been a Professor of International Tax Law at the Institute for Austrian and International Tax Law of WU (Vienna University of Economics and Business) since 2020. He also serves, *inter alia*, as the chairman of the CFE ECJ Task Force.

Prof. Dr DDr h.c. **Michael Lang** is Head of the Institute for Austrian and International Tax Law at WU (Vienna University of Economics and Business) and has been a professor there since 1994. He is also the Academic Director of the LLM Program in International Tax Law and the Doctoral Program in International Business Taxation (DIBT) at WU.

Prof. Dr Dr mult. h.c. **Pasquale Pistone** holds the Ad Personam Jean Monnet Chair on European Tax Law and Policy at the Institute for Austrian and International Tax Law of WU (Vienna University of Economics and Business). He is also the Academic Chair of IBFD, Amsterdam, and a Full Professor of Tax Law at the University of Salerno. Furthermore, he is professor honoris causa at the Ural State Law University, Russia; at the University of Cape Town, South Africa; and doctor honoris causa at the University of Örebro, Sweden.

Prof. Dr **Alexander Rust** has been a Professor of International Tax Law at the Institute for Austrian and International Tax Law of WU (Vienna University of Economics and Business) since 2014. Before joining the Institute, he held the position of Acting Assistant Professor in the International Tax Program at New York University and the positions of Professor of Tax Law and Director of the Master's Program in European and International Tax Law at the University of Luxembourg.

Prof. Dr **Josef Schuch** has been a Professor of International Tax Law at the Institute for Austrian and International Tax Law of WU (Vienna University of Economics and Business) since 2002. He is a tax advisor and partner of Deloitte Österreich.

Prof. Dr **Karoline Spies** has been a Professor of Value Added Tax Law at the Institute for Austrian and International Tax Law of WU (Vienna University of Economics and Business) since 2020. She also works as a Tax Manager at Deloitte Österreich.

Prof. Dr **Claus Staringer** has been a Professor of Tax Law at the Institute for Austrian and International Tax Law of WU (Vienna University of Economics and Business) since 2003. He was also a partner with the international law firm Freshfields Bruckhaus Deringer.

Assoc. Prof. PD Dr **Rita Szudoczky** has been an Associate Professor of Tax Law at the Institute for Austrian and International Tax Law of WU (Vienna University of Economics and Business) since 2022. She obtained her PhD degree at the Amsterdam Centre for Tax Law, University of Amsterdam in 2013. Rita had previously worked for the IBFD as well as for different law firms in the Netherlands and Hungary. She has been delegated by Hungary to the List of Independent Persons of Standing for the EU Arbitration Convention and the EU Dispute Resolution Directive.

Contributors

Benjamin Beer is a Teaching and Research Associate at the Institute for Austrian and International Tax Law of WU (Vienna University of Economics and Business). He holds a master's degree in business law. Before joining the institute, he was employed as an audit associate at PwC Austria.

Juliane Beverungen is a Teaching and Research Associate at the Institute for Austrian and International Tax Law of WU (Vienna University of Economics and Business). She holds a bachelor's degree in economics and a bachelor's degree in political science from the Albert-Ludwigs-University Freiburg and is pursuing a master's degree in accounting and taxation at WU. Before joining the Institute, she was employed as a Tax Associate at KPMG Austria.

Prof. Dr **Daniel W. Blum**, LLM (NYU) is a Visiting Professor at the Institute for Austrian and International Tax Law of WU (Vienna University of Economics and Business) and a senior tax manager at Deloitte Vienna.

Timoleon Angelos Christodoulopoulos is a Teaching and Research Associate at the Institute for Austrian and International Tax Law of WU (Vienna University of Economics and Business). He holds a bachelor's degree in law from DUTH (Democritus University of Thrace), a master's degree in commercial and corporate law from QMUL (Queen Mary University of London), and a master's degree in international tax law from WU. He has worked as an international tax advisor in Luxembourg and Greece.

Eric Coenen is a Teaching and Research Associate at the Institute for Austrian and International Tax Law of WU (Vienna University of Economics and Business). He holds a master's degree in business law.

Bence Péter Komár is a Teaching and Research Associate at the Institute for Austrian and International Tax Law of WU (Vienna University of Economics and Business). He holds a bachelor's and a master's degree in business law from WU. Before joining the institute, he worked as a paralegal at a Vienna-based business law firm.

Dominic Krenn is a Freshfields Research Project Associate at the Institute for Austrian and International Tax Law of WU (Vienna University of Economics and Business). He holds a bachelor's and a master's degree in business law from WU. Before joining the institute, he did several internships in law firms in Austria and abroad.

Yasmin Lawson is a PwC Research Project Associate at the Institute for Austrian and International Tax Law and a doctoral candidate at WU (Vienna University of Economics and Business). She holds a master's degree in business law.

Giuseppe Moramarco is a Teaching and Research Associate and PhD candidate in the Doctoral Program in International Business Taxation (DIBT) at the Institute for Austrian and International Tax Law of WU (Vienna University of Economics and Business). He holds a master's degree in law, a master's degree in tax law, and an LLM in international tax law from WU. He worked for several years as a lawyer specializing in international and EU tax law for international law firms.

Kilian Posch is a Teaching and Research Associate at the Institute for Austrian and International Tax Law of WU (Vienna University of Economics and Business). He holds a law degree and a bachelor's degree in economics from the University of Graz. Prior to becoming a Teaching and Research Associate, he was employed in a tax advisory and was a student assistant for tax law.

Iris Tschatsch is a Teaching and Research Associate at the Institute for Austrian and International Tax Law and a doctoral candidate at WU (Vienna University of Economics and Business). She holds a bachelor's degree in business administration and a master's degree in taxation and obtained her LLM in International Tax Law at WU in 2023.

Dr **Gustavo Weiss de Resende**, LLM, is a Postdoctoral Teaching and Research Fellow at the Institute for Austrian and International Tax Law at the Vienna University of Economics and Business. He earned his PhD from the Max-Planck Institute for Tax Law and Public Finance and the Ludwig-Maximilians University in Germany while also serving as an Academic Visitor at the Centre for Business Taxation at the University of Oxford in England. He obtained his LLM in international and European business law with a focus on international taxation from the LMU in Munich. He also has experience working for international organizations such as the OECD and the European Commission.

Summary of Contents

Summary of Contents

Preface

The Vienna Convention on The Law of Treaties (VCLT) is a pivotal instrument in the field of international law and establishes the rules governing the conclusion, interpretation, and termination of treaties. Its relevance extends beyond the general scope of international relations, permeating various specialized areas such as tax law. In particular, the VCLT is a crucial factor in guiding the interpretation of tax treaties. Courts and authorities frequently consult the interpretation principles codified in the VCLT for tax treaty interpretation, even though the VCLT itself is just a treaty under international public law and, as such, has the same status as a DTC. Thus far, minimal research has focused on its impact on interpreting and applying tax treaties.

To analyse the VCLT's interpretation rules in Articles 31-33 and their relevance for tax treaty interpretation, the 31st Viennese Symposium on International Tax Law was held on 17 June 2024 at WU (Vienna University of Economics and Business). Renowned professors from Austrian and foreign universities, tax researchers from the WU, and tax experts from various countries participated in the symposium. The speakers have since completed contributions using input received during it, and these have become the chapters of this book. Each author offers an in-depth analysis along with the most recent scientific research on their topic.

The editors would like to thank Caroline Ristic, Christina Sudrat, Myriam Pereira de Milinic, and Michael Hubmann who were the primary people responsible for organizing the symposium and made essential contributions to the preparation and publication of this book. The editors would also like to thank all of the authors who have patiently revised their contributions in order to enhance the quality of the book, and Jenny Hill who contributed greatly with her linguistic editing of the authors' texts.

Above all, sincere thanks to the publishing house Wolters Kluwer for agreeing to include this publication in their catalogue and for excellent cooperation.

Georg Kofler
Michael Lang
Pasquale Pistone
Alexander Rust
Josef Schuch
Karoline Spies
Claus Staringer
Rita Szudoczky

CHAPTER 1

The Relevance of the Vienna Convention on the Law of Treaties for Tax Treaty Interpretation

Michael Lang & Kilian Posch

1 CAN INTERPRETATION BE REGULATED?

Every text requires interpretation. It is well-established in hermeneutics that no word, sentence, or paragraph has a singular, timeless, and objective meaning that could be derived irrespective of the context in which it exists.[1] Instead, meaning must be uncovered by virtue of interpretation which is not only a passive process but also a productive act by the interpreters.[2] This holds true for tax treaties just as for any other legal document as they are based on language. Therefore, the role of interpretation in applying tax treaties cannot be overstated. It invokes the question, however, if practitioners, academics, and judges must adhere to a certain way of interpreting the law and apply certain interpretational methods to determine the meaning of a

1. Hans-Georg Gadamer, *Wahrheit und Methode: Grundzüge einer Philosophischen Hermeneutik* 280 (Mohr Siebeck 1990); Bernd Rüthers et al., *Rechtstheorie und juristische Methodenlehre* 111 et seq. (C.H. Beck 11th ed. 2020); Thomas Vesting, *Legal Theory* 110 et seq. (C.H. Beck 2018).
2. Rüthers et al., *supra* n. 1, at 113.

provision. For international treaties between states pursuant to Article 1 Vienna Convention on the Law of Treaties (VCLT),[3] Articles 31, 32, and 33 VCLT codify rules for their interpretation. These are often considered in international tax cases and exert influence on the interpretation of tax provisions not only by the significantly more than 100 current parties to the VCLT[4] but at least in the case of Article 31 and Article 32 VCLT also as customary international law (CIL).[5]

Before detailing the rules of interpretation themselves, it must be clarified what the actual purpose is of interpretation. Generally, its objective is to find the regulation's meaning from the inherently imprecise language with which it is expressed.[6] To ascertain meaning, interpreters first consider the wording of the law and its nuances, put the provision in its context, evaluate its object and purpose, and take into account its genesis. These are 'ingredients' of interpretation that are overwhelmingly acknowledged irrespective of disputes in legal theory concerning the subject of legal interpretation[7] and are also used when interpretation is not legally regulated.[8] Even in the absence of interpretation rules, therefore, a meaningful constraint of interpreters is the object of interpretation itself, to find the true meaning of the law and thus the adherence to the principle of legality.[9] Interpretation methods cannot be used to defeat the purpose of interpretation from the outset.[10] It is central to it that the meaning attributed to the law by the interpreter should be compatible with what legislators are required to accept for or against themselves considering the legal formulation that they

3. For details on the scope of the VCLT, *see* Kirsten Schmalenbach, *Article 1. Scope of the Present Convention, in Vienna Convention on the Law of Treaties* (Oliver Dörr & Kirsten Schmalenbach eds, Springer Berlin Heidelberg 2018).
4. United Nations Treaty Collections, https://treaties.un.org/doc/Publication/MTDSG/Volume%2 0II/Chapter%20XXIII/XXIII-1.en.pdf, 14 March 2024.
5. Philip Baker, *Chapter 3: The Localization of Tax Treaty Interpretation, in Building Global International Tax Law: Essays in Honour of Guglielmo Maisto* 47 (IBFD 2022).
6. *See* Andrei Marmor, *Interpretation and Legal Theory* 9 et seq. (Hart 2d ed. 2005), who also delves into the related question of what actually is the meaning of (legal) philosophy.
7. In legal theory, there is a dispute on what the true meaning of law constitutes. According to intentionalism, which is akin to the subjective theory in German legal tradition, the legislative intent inside and outside of the normative text is a major factor for finding the meaning of law; *see* Marmor, *supra* n. 6, at 119 et seq.; for the German tradition, *see* Bernd Rüthers, *Methodenrealismus in Jurisprudenz und Justiz*, 61 JZ 53 (2006) https://doi.org/10.1628/002268806775435575; *see also* Karl Larenz & Claus-Wilhelm Canaris, *Methodenlehre der Rechtswissenschaft* 153 et seq. (Springer 3d ed. 1995). The school of textualism (and the German school of objective theory), however, stipulates that the intent of the law is directly coming from the legal text – legislative intent beyond what can be found in the written law itself is not to be considered for interpretative purposes; *see* for the German tradition Karl Engisch, *Einführung in das juristische Denken* 161 et seq. (W. Kohlhammer 11th ed. 2010); Karl Larenz, *Methodenlehre der Rechtswissenschaft* 316 et seq. (Springer 6th ed. 1991). Historical documents are thus of less interpretative value to them. This is, of course, a simplified depiction of legal theories as intentionalism alone can be divided into several sub-branches.
8. *See also* Michael Lang, *Can Law Regulate Its Own Interpretation? Relevance and Meaning of Articles 31-33 of the Vienna Convention of the Law of Treaties (VCLT) and Article 3 Para. 2 of the Model Convention of the Organisation of Economic Co-Operation and Development (OECD MC) for the Interpretation of Double-Taxation Conventions, in Research Handbook on International Taxation* 174 (Yariv Brauner ed., Edward Elgar Publishing Limited 2020).
9. *See* Larenz, *supra* n. 7, at 247, who views the principle of legality as the most important boundary for interpretation by judges.
10. Michael Potacs, *Rechtstheorie* 155 et seq. (Facultas 2. Auflage ed. 2019).

chose and that came into force.[11] It is this finding of meaning in the necessarily ambiguous written language that defines interpretation. This holds true irrespective of the legal tradition with which someone sympathizes. Interpretation that does not aim to find what is or can reasonably be the meaning of the provision is not grounded in legality and the principles of legal science.

What role remains, then, for interpretation provisions such as Articles 31-33 VCLT? These rules constitute written law and are therefore a component of the legal body that must be applied. Nonetheless, there is no way for a legislator to ascertain that the interpretation provisions themselves are interpreted as they intended. After all, interpretation rules are also expressed by means of language and thus require interpretation.[12] In the process of finding the meaning of the interpretation provisions, practitioners can hardly rely on the application of the very rules for which they set out to find the meaning; the interpretation rules are the product of their own interpretation and not their starting point. Hence, it must be concluded that interpretation of the law cannot be fully and conclusively regulated. Some discretion still remains even in the presence of codified interpretation rules. This also results from the fact that legal methodology is routed in the conception of language itself that is not accessible to full regulation.[13]

It should also be remembered that the regulation of interpretation has never been a purely technical issue but is rather a political one.[14] The historical purpose of the interpretation rules originating in the nineteenth century was to limit the power of judges when applying the law.[15] The VCLT rules can also be viewed in this light as distributing the power of interpretation between interpreters and states. For example, the seeming subsidiarity of historical documents[16] is compatible with the interest of contracting parties to not commit themselves to one specific interpretation at the time of the treaty's conclusion. Instead, opportunity is afforded for later influence on the meaning of the provisions.[17] Eventually, however, judges decide on the interpretation of the law, and it is encompassed within their competence to also interpret the applicable interpretation rules.

2 INTERPRETATION METHODS IN THE VCLT AND THEIR RANKING

The interpretation rules in the VCLT were never intended to build a rigorous canon of interpretation. Rather, they were an attempt to codify the methods that were already in use at the time and find a pragmatic compromise between different theoretical

11. *Ibid.*; Franz Reimer, *Juristische Methodenlehre* 249 (Nomos 2d ed. 2020).
12. Lang, *supra* n. 8, at 175.
13. Christiane Wendehorst, *Methodennormen in Kontinentaleuropäischen Kodifikationen*, 75 RabelsZ 734 (2011).
14. Reimer, *supra* n. 11, at 40 et seq.
15. Christiane Wendehorst, *Methodenlehre und Privatrecht in Europa*, *in Vom praktischen Wert der Methode* 833 (Clemens Jabloner et al. eds, Manz 2011); *see also* Lang, *supra* n. 8, at 175 et seq.
16. For details, *see* s. 2 of this chapter.
17. Lang, *supra* n. 8, at 175 et seq.

approaches.[18] Accordingly, Article 31(1) VCLT features the most common means of interpretation and reads as follows: '1. A treaty shall be interpreted in good faith in accordance with the ordinary meaning to be given to the terms of the treaty in their context and in the light of its object and purpose.'

This general rule of interpretation encompasses the ordinary meaning, corresponding to the grammatical interpretation method; the context, matching the systematic method; and the object and purpose, relating to the teleological method of interpretation.[19] All of these methods must be used in good faith thereby restricting the interpreter from willingly diverging from the 'true' meaning of the norm.[20] According to the VCLT's travaux préparatoires, Article 31(1) entails no ranking among the featured interpretation methods: The same importance is given to the ordinary meaning as to the context or object and purpose of the treaty.[21] The equal ranking is not undisputed by scholars of legal theory. While the majority of academics are in favour of interpretation methods being of equal status,[22] there are proponents for a ranking of methods for which certain approaches are only engaged if more straightforward methods, most notably the grammatical and systematic interpretation, yield no adequate result.[23]

The VCLT does not seem to support an application of *all* interpretation methods with no interrelating hierarchies either. Even though the VCLT's interpretation rules are a pragmatic compromise between different schools of thought, the International Law Commission (ILC) was approaching the draft for the interpretation provisions from a textualist standpoint, i.e., the text of a treaty should be considered the expression of the parties' intention.[24] Historical materials, however, were deemed less authentic and thus supplementary.[25] Concordantly, Article 32 VCLT, dubbed 'supplementary means of interpretation', suggests a subsidiary role for the historical method for treaty interpretation over the rest of the standard methods:

> Recourse may be had to supplementary means of interpretation, including the preparatory work of the treaty and the circumstances of its conclusion, in order to confirm the meaning resulting from the application of article 31, or to determine the meaning when the interpretation according to article 31:
>
> (a) leaves the meaning ambiguous or obscure; or

18. Oliver Dörr, *Art 31. General Rule of Interpretation, in Vienna Convention on the Law of Treaties* 560 (Oliver Dörr & Kirsten Schmalenbach eds, Springer Berlin Heidelberg 2018).
19. *Ibid.*, at 579 et seq.
20. Heribert Franz Köck, *Vertragsinterpretation und Vertragsrechtskonvention: zur Bedeutung d. Art. 31 u. 32 d. Wiener Vertragsrechtskonvention 1969* 85 et seq. (Duncker und Humblot 1st ed. 1976).
21. ILC, *Draft Articles on the Law of Treaties with Commentaries, in Yearbook of the International Law Commission*, Vol. II, 219 et seq. (United Nations ed. 1966).
22. Larenz, *supra* n. 7, at 343 et seq.
23. In German literature most famously Franz Bydlinski, *Juristische Methodenlehre und Rechtsbegriff* 558-565 (Springer 2d ed. 1982).
24. ILC, VCLT Final Draft, Commentary to Art. 27, 220; Dörr, *Art 31. General Rule of Interpretation, in Vienna Convention on the Law of Treaties, supra* n. 18, at 560 et seq.; *see also Libya v. Chad* ICJ Reports (1994) 6.
25. Gustavo Weiss de Resende, *Supplementary Means of Interpretation (Art 32 VCLT) and Tax Treaty Interpretation*, Chapter 8 in this book.

to note that the power received by non-DSNs from MCO decays decreases with distance. To reduce the charging time and maintain energy balance among the nodes following the charging process, it becomes necessary to calculate the anchor point through calculation, which determines the specific positioning of the MCO.

Algorithm 1: Algorithms for determining DSN

Input: $S = \{s_1, s_2, ..., s_N\}$, network region size L
Output: the set of clusters C and the corresponding DSN and non-DSNs
set the density bandwidth parameter $B = L$
set the clustering set $C_1 = S, C = \{C_1\}$
the node closest to the center of network is selected as DSN
while $\exists\{C_i \in C, ndsn_{i,j} \in C_i\}, d(ndsn_{i,j}, C_i) > R_{trans}$ **do**
  $B = B - \Delta b$
  for *node in S* **do**
    Calculate the mean-shift vector of this node based on the bandwidth B
    Move the node to a new position based on the mean-shift vector
    Repeat until the mean-shift vector converges to 0
  end
  Obtain the new clustering set $C = \{C_1, C_2, ...C_{K_{DSN}}\}$
  $\forall C_i \in C$, the node closest to the clustering center in C_i is selected as the DSN
  $\forall ndsn_{i,j} \in C_i$, calculate $d(ndsn_{i,j}, C_i)$
end
return the set of clusters C and and the corresponding DSN and non-DSN

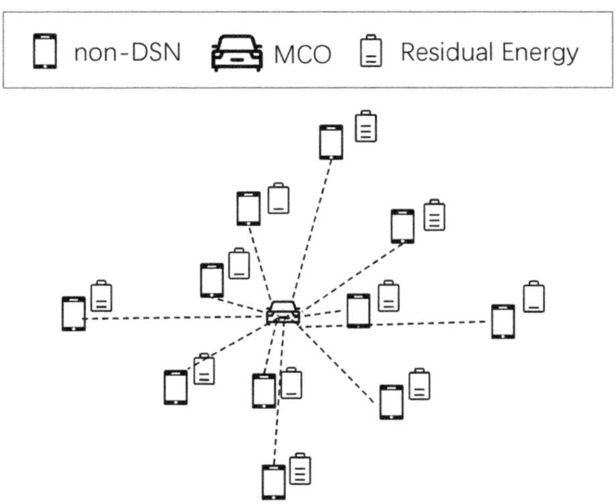

Figure 2. Energy distribution of non-DSNs.

In this paper, non-DSNs with varying residual energies are represented as discrete particles with distinct masses. Nodes with higher residual energy correspond to particles with lower masses. The task of identifying the anchor point for each cluster can be converted into the problem of locating the center of mass within a two-dimensional region.

The coordinates of the anchor point can be obtained through the following procedure:

$$E_{C_i'}^{total} = \sum_{ndsn_{i,j}' \in C_i'} \left(EC_{sensor} - E_{ndsn_{i,j}'}^{res} \right), \tag{46}$$

$$E_{C_i'}^{y} = \sum_{ndsn'_{i,j} \in C_i'} \left(EC_{sensor} - E_{ndsn'_{i,j}}^{res} \right) \times x_{ndsn'_{i,j}}, \tag{47}$$

$$E_{C_i'}^{x} = \sum_{ndsn'_{i,j} \in C_i'} \left(EC_{sensor} - E_{ndsn'_{i,j}}^{res} \right) \times y_{ndsn'_{i,j}}, \tag{48}$$

$$\left(x_{C_i'}^{p}, y_{C_i'}^{p} \right) = \left(\frac{E_{C_i'}^{y}}{E_{C_i'}^{total}}, \frac{E_{C_i'}^{x}}{E_{C_i'}^{total}} \right), \tag{49}$$

where $E_{C_i'}^{total}$ is the total energy consumed by all non-DSNs in C_i', $\left(x_{ndsn'_{i,j}}, y_{ndsn'_{i,j}} \right)$ is the coordinates of $ndsn'_{i,j}$, $E_{C_i'}^{y}$ is the sum of static torques of all non-DSNs in the cluster along the y-axis, $E_{C_i'}^{x}$ is the sum of static torques of all non-DSNs along the x-axis, and $\left(x_{C_i'}^{p}, y_{C_i'}^{p} \right)$ is the location of the anchoring point where the MCO stops.

When the node distribution is uneven or the network topology is irregular, our proposed mean-shift-based clustering algorithm will tend to divide denser areas into clusters as well as reduce the number of clusters to be divided.

4.2. Scheduling for MCs

4.2.1. Scheduling for MCD

This paper presents a periodic scheduling scheme that comprises two distinct parts: the initial cycle and the general cycle.

In the initial cycle, as depicted in Figure 3, the MCD arrives at the DSN in C_i at time a_{C_i}. To maintain the periodic variation of energy and data within the node, it is necessary for the MCD to undergo a waiting period at the DSN in C_i for a duration of x_{C_i}. Subsequently, the MCD proceeds to replenish energy for the DSN in C_i until it reaches full capacity. The charging time, denoted as $t_{C_i}^{c\_1}$, is calculated using the following equation:

$$t_{C_i}^{c\_1} = \frac{(a_{C_i} + x_{C_i}) \times E_{rx}(|nDSN_i \times G|)}{P_{C_i}}. \tag{50}$$

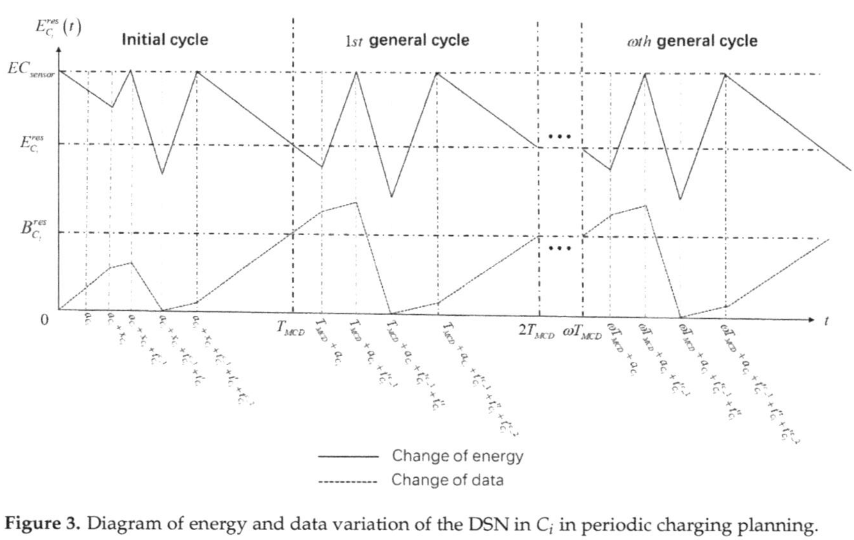

Figure 3. Diagram of energy and data variation of the DSN in C_i in periodic charging planning.

Following the first charging phase, the MCD collects the accumulated data stored in the DSN in C_i. The duration of time, denoted as $t^t_{C_i}$, required for data collection is calculated through the utilization of the following equation:

$$t^t_{C_i} = \frac{(a_{C_i} + x_{C_i}) \times (|nDSN_i| + 1) \times G + t^{c\_1}_{C_i} \times G}{Q - G}. \tag{51}$$

To fully charge the DSN in C_i, the MCD commences another charging process. The duration of the charging time, represented as $t^{c\_2}_{C_i}$, can be calculated using the following equation or methodology:

$$t^{c\_2}_{C_i} = \frac{t^t_{C_i} \times E_{tx}(Q, d(C_i, MCD))}{P_{C_i}}. \tag{52}$$

In the general cycle, the arrival time of MCD at the DSN in C_i is $\omega T_{DSN} + a_{C_i}$. The MCD does not have to wait and directly charges the DSN to full charge. The charging time $t'^{c\_1}_{C_i}$ is calculated as follows:

$$t'^{c\_1}_{C_i} = \frac{\left(T_{DSN} - \left(a_{C_i} + x_{C_i} + t^t_{C_i} + t^{c\_1}_{C_i} + t^{c\_2}_{C_i}\right) + a_{C_i}\right) \times E_{rx}(|nDSN_i| \times G)}{P_{C_i}}. \tag{53}$$

The time $t'^t_{C_i}$ to collect data is calculated as follows:

$$t'^t_{C_i} = \frac{\left(T_{DSN} - \left(a_{C_i} + x_{C_i} + t^t_{C_i} + t^{c\_1}_{C_i} + t^{c\_2}_{C_i}\right) + a_{C_i}\right) \times (|nDSN_i| + 1) \times G + \left(t'^{c\_1}_{C_i} + t^{c\_2}_{C_i}\right) \times G}{Q - G}. \tag{54}$$

Finally, the time $t'^{c\_2}_{C_i}$ to fully charge the DSN in C_i again is calculated as follows:

$$t'^{c\_2}_{C_i} = \frac{t'^t_{C_i} \times E_{tx}(Q, d(C_i, MCD))}{P_{C_i}}. \tag{55}$$

To maintain periodic variations in the energy and data of the DSN, it is necessary to ensure that the total time of the initial and general cycles is equal, denoted as $t^{c\_1}_{C_i} + t^t_{C_i} + t^{c\_2}_{C_i} + x_{C_i} = t'^{c\_1}_{C_i} + t'^t_{C_i} + t'^{c\_2}_{C_i}$. In order to achieve this, we can formulate a K-element equation:

$$\begin{array}{c} t^{c\_1}_{C_1} + t^t_{C_1} + t^{c\_2}_{C_1} + x_{C_1} = t'^{c\_1}_{C_1} + t'^t_{C_1} + t'^{c\_2}_{C_1} \\ t^{c\_1}_{C_2} + t^t_{C_2} + t^{c\_2}_{C_2} + x_{C_2} = t'^{c\_1}_{C_2} + t'^t_{C_2} + t'^{c\_2}_{C_2} \\ \vdots \\ t^{c\_1}_{C_i} + t^t_{C_i} + t^{c\_2}_{C_i} + x_{C_i} = t'^{c\_1}_{C_i} + t'^t_{C_i} + t'^{c\_2}_{C_i} \\ \vdots \\ t^{c\_1}_{C_{KDSN}} + t^t_{C_{KDSN}} + t^{c\_2}_{C_{KDSN}} + x_{C_{KDSN}} = t'^{c\_1}_{C_{KDSN}} + t'^{c}_{C_{KDSN}} + t'^{c\_2}_{C_{KDSN}} \end{array}. \tag{56}$$

This equation is guaranteed to have a unique solution, and the solution x_{C_i} represents the waiting time for the initial cycle of the DSN in C_i.

The scheduling problem of periodic joint energy replenishment and data collection can be effectively addressed through the utilization of a hybrid particle swarm algorithm (HPSA). The HPSA combines the principles of particle swarm optimization (PSO) and genetic algorithms (GAs) to optimize the scheduling process thoroughly.

In order to mitigate the common issue of falling into local optima inherent in PSO, this study introduces a mutation operation inspired by genetic algorithms. By introducing random into the swarm, this operation enables the exploration of alternative solutions beyond the immediate neighborhood, thus enhancing the algorithm's ability to escape local optima.

Consequently, the proposed hybrid particle swarm optimization algorithm encompasses the following stages:

(1) Initialization: The particle swarm is initialized with randomly generated solutions.
(2) Equations Substitution: Appropriate variable substitutions are made in the Equation (56) to calculate the waiting time, charging time, and data collection time.
(3) Optimal Solution Determination: The optimal solution within the population is determined by evaluating each particle.
(4) Position Update and Mutation: The positions of the particles are updated based on their velocities, and the mutation operation is applied to introduce diversity into the swarm.

The specific algorithm flow is detailed in Algorithm 2.

Algorithm 2: scheduling algorithm for MCD

Input: number of iterations P, factor of updating c_1, factor of mutating c_2, and infomation of DSNs
Output: the charging sequence, charging time and data transfer time of MCD
Initialize the particle swarm $d_1, d_2, ..., d_s(d_i = \{l_1, l_2, ..., l_r\})$, randomly generate paths, and substitute into the Equation (57) to calculate the waiting time
for *i = 1:P* **do**
  for *j = 1:s* **do**
    for *t = 1:r* **do**
      $rate_1 = random(0,1)$
      if $rate_1 > c_1$ **then**
        updating the particle d_j to get closer to the population optimal solution
      end
      $rate_2 = random(0,1)$
      if $rate_2 > c_2$ **then**
        mutate the position d_j
      end
    end
    recalculate the waiting time by substituting the new particle $d_j^{'}$ into the equation
    if *the new particle* $d_j^{'}$ *is not superior to the particle* d_j **then**
      restore the new particle to d_j
    end
  end
  Select the optimal particle in the population:
  (1) Select the particle with the fewest node deaths.
  (2) Select the particle with the minimum data overflow among the remaining particles.
  (3) Select the particle with the lowest delay among the remaining particles as the optimal particle in the population.
end
return the charging sequence, charging time and data transfer time of MCD

4.2.2. Scheduling of MCO

Since non-DSNs consume much less energy than DSNs, they can tolerate longer charging delays. Moreover, to extend the lifetime of nodes, we adopt a strategy where the nodes in each cluster are fully charged when the MCO reaches the anchor point, which can achieve the long network lifetime [12].

Similar to the scheduling of MCDs, we employ the hybrid particle swarm algorithm to address the scheduling problem of MCOs. We propose the following modifications to the selection process for determining the optimal particle in the population:

(1) Select the particle with the fewest node deaths.
(2) Select the particle with the smallest delay among the remaining particles.

It is important to highlight the distinction between the MCO and the periodic scheduling of the MCD. The scheduling for each cycle is not identical, and at the start of each cycle, it is necessary to reassess anchor points based on the remaining energy of non-DSNs and devise a new path plan.

4.3. Time Complexity of the Proposed Algorithm

We use the mean-shift algorithm to determine the DSNs and the anchor points for MCO. As for [29], the time complexity of the mean-shift algorithm is $O(n^2)$, where n is the number of nodes participating in clustering. For determining the DSNs, the number of nodes in clustering is N, which is the total number of nodes. Assuming a total of T_1 iterations are required, the time complexity is $O(N^2) \times T_1$. For determining the anchor points for the MCO, the number of nodes in clustering is $N - K_{DSN}$. When calculating anchor points based on energy distribution, it is necessary to calculate the energy of each point. Therefore, the time complexity of this part is $O(N - K_{DSN})$. Assuming a total of T_2 iterations are required, the time complexity is $O((N - K_{DSN})^2) \times T_2 + O(N - K_{DSN})$.

The time complexity for scheduling MCDs primarily depends on the number of iterations, the number of particles, and the number of DSNs in the hybrid particle swarm algorithm. Assume that the algorithm iterates P_1 times and the number of particles is n_1. When calculating the optimal particle in the population, we need to solve the K-element equation for each particle to calculate the residence time of MCDs, and then compare the current particle with the best particle in the population. When solving the equation, we use the LU decomposition method with a time complexity of $O((K_{DSN})^3)$ [30], while the comparison of particle require a time complexity of $O(1)$. Therefore, the time complexity for calculating the optimal particle in the population is $O(n_1 \times (K_{DSN})^3)$. For particle update and mutation operations, as we need to operate on each position of each particle, the time complexity is $O(n_1 \times K_{DSN})$. The time complexity for other operations of the hybrid particle swarm algorithm is $O(1)$ and can be ignored. Therefore, the time complexity of scheduling MCDs is $(O(n_1 \times (K_{DSN})^3) + O(n_1 \times K_{DSN})) \times P_1$. We assume that when scheduling MCOs, the hybrid particle swarm algorithm iterates P_2 times with a particle count of n_2, and no equations need to be calculated when scheduling MCOs. Therefore, its time complexity is as follows: $(O(n_2 \times K_{nDSN})) \times P_2$.

5. Performance Evaluation

5.1. Simulation Environment

In this paper, we evaluate the performance of our proposed scheme by comparing it with the JERDC scheme proposed in [11], the SPSS scheme proposed in [12], the DGCS scheme proposed in [31] and the scheme proposed in [32]. It is worth noting that in [32], we used a combination of the most effective CIBA algorithm and the MDSA algorithm, referred to as the CIBA-MDSA scheme. The JERDC scheme proposed in [11] selects DSNs based on their remaining energy and their distances to their own clustering centers, and deploys two MCs to traverse along the shortest Hamiltonian cycle consisting of all the DSNs in order to collaboratively perform the energy replenishment and data collection tasks. The SPSS scheme proposed in [12] selects the DSNs by considering the sensor's indegree, distance to neighbors, and residual energy. It uses a genetic algorithm to obtain the path with the highest charging utility, and then divides it into two paths of the same length, traversing both paths simultaneously using two MCs. The CIBA-MDSA scheme [32] uses the location of each node and the intersection of a circle with each node as the center and the charging range as the radius as candidate anchor points. The node with the highest indegree among the candidate anchor points is selected as the anchor point until all nodes are covered. In addition to this, the CIBA-MDSA scheme uses the indegree of the anchor point and the distance from the anchor point to the BS to determine the path for the MC to access the anchor point. The DGCS scheme proposed in [31] first divides the sensor nodes into clusters using the circle covering method and determines the anchor points. The minimum number of MCs is then determined using the elbow method in the k-means algorithm. Finally, a genetic algorithm is used to schedule the MCs for node charging and data collection.

For the selection of MCD and MCO speed, when the speed of the MC rises, its traveling energy consumption rises and the charging delay will show a decreasing trend within a certain range. Whereas the energy of the MC is limited, a rise in its traveling energy consumption will result in a decrease in the proportion of the MC's capacity used for charging, leading to the MC only being able to charge fewer nodes. Therefore, when the speed of MC continues to increase, the energy consumption of MC for traveling increases, but the charging delay decreases instead. Considering the other side, when the speed of the MC decreases, the traveling power of the MC decreases, but the time taken by the MC to travel the same distance rises. When the power decreases and time rises, the energy consumed by the MC traveling is unknown. Therefore, we chose 1 m/s for our MCD and MCO speeds based on experience as well as references [33–35].

Moreover, in the simulation experiments, nodes are deployed in the sensor network by randomization. Therefore, the distribution of nodes may be uniform or non-uniform. Our experimental results demonstrate that our clustering algorithm can effectively handle non-regular topology networks and non-uniformly distributed nodes.

We conducted three sets of simulation experiments to evaluate the performance of our proposed scheme, the JERDC scheme, the SPSS scheme, the CIBA-MDSA scheme, and the DGCS scheme based on the size of the simulation region, the number of nodes and the data sense rate of nodes, respectively, with each set of experiments running for 50 cycles of simulation. Moreover, three criteria are used to present the performance of these algorithms:

(1) Average delay. The network's data collection delay and the DSN's charging delay are equal to the duration of the MCD charging cycle, while the charging delay of the non-DSN nodes is equal to the duration of the MCO charging cycle. The average delay is a crucial metric in the joint energy replenishment and data collection optimization scenario [12], which represents the timeliness of network data collection and charging.
(2) Charging efficiency: It is the ratio of the energy used by the MC for charging sensors to the total energy consumed by the MC. This metric measures how efficiently the MC utilizes its energy resources to charge the sensor nodes within the network [36].
(3) Average residual energy of nodes: It is the average residual energy of all nodes at the end of the simulation. A larger average residual energy among all nodes when the simulation is terminated indicates a longer network lifetime. This metric is used to evaluate the performance of the energy efficiency in WRSNs [12].

The parameters used in the simulation are shown in Table 3.

Table 3. Simulation parameters.

Parameter	Value
E_{elec}	50×10^{-9} J/bit [26]
ϵ_{mp}	0.0013×10^{-12} J/bit/m^4 [26]
ϵ_{fs}	1×10^{-11} J/bit/m^2 [26]
E_{sense}	45×10^{-9} J/bit/ [16]
G	[32 bit/s, 64 bit/s, 96 bit/s, 128 bit/s, 160 bit/s]
α	0.64 [27]
β	30 [27]
P_{charge}	50 W [20]
V_{mc}	1 m/s [33–35]
P_{move}	10 W
R_{trans}	120 m [37]
R_{charge}	40 m [12]
d_0	92 m [37]
L	[300 m, 350 m, 400 m, 450 m, 500 m]
N	[300, 350, 400, 450, 500]
E_{mc}	18 KJ
E_{sensor}	4 J
Q	100 KB/s
B_{mc}	10 MB
B_{sensor}	2 MB

5.2. Performance Analysis

5.2.1. Varying the Size of Simulation Region

In Figure 4, we set the size of simulation region to 300 m, 350 m, 400 m, 450 m, and 500 m, the number of nodes to 400, and the data sense rate of nodes to 128 bit/s. We set the size of the simulation region as the horizontal coordinates of the figures.

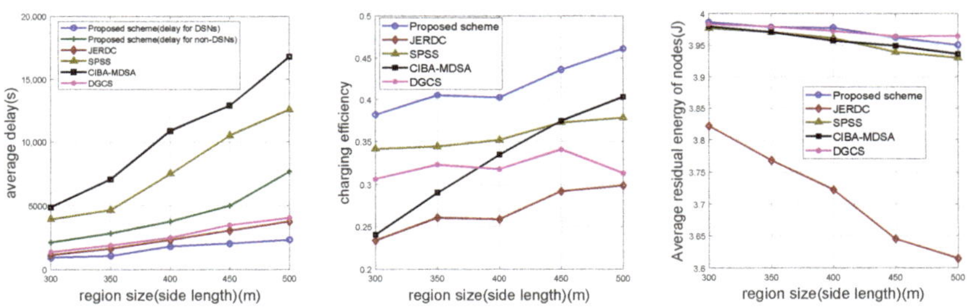

(a) (b) (c)

Figure 4. Impact of the size of simulation region. Where (**a**) depicts the simulation results of average delay, (**b**) depicts the simulation results of charging efficiency and (**c**) shows the simulation results of nodes' average residual energy.

Figure 4a presents a clear trend where the average delay of all schemes experiences an increment as the region size is varied from 300 m to 500 m. This increase in delay can be primarily ascribed to the expansion of the region, which leads to a higher number of anchor points. The increased number of anchor points, in turn, lengthens the path length traversed by the MCs. Significantly, within the proposed scheme, the delay of DSNs attains the lowest value among all the schemes under consideration. This indicates that the network data collection delay of the proposed scheme is also the minimum. The underlying reason for this favorable outcome lies in the utilization of the communication radius instead of the charging radius during the selection of DSNs. This substitution effectively reduces the number of anchor points associated with the MCD, thereby reducing the travel distance of the MCD. Concerning the non-DSNs, their delay is slightly higher than that of the JERDC scheme but remains notably lower than the other two schemes. The relatively low delay of the JERDC scheme can be attributed to its employment of two MCs to partially charge the nodes along the shortest Hamiltonian cycle, which effectively curtails the delay. In contrast, the DGCS scheme deploys a greater number of MCs to serve the nodes, achieving a lower delay as well. Nevertheless, it is crucial to note that the network data collection delays of both the JERDC and DGCS schemes exceed that of the proposed scheme. The SPSS scheme and the CIBA-MDSA scheme exhibit higher delays, primarily because the delay factor was not incorporated into their path planning processes. When evaluating the rate of increase in delay, the delay of DSNs in the proposed scheme grows at a slower pace. This can be explained by the fact that, as the simulation area expands, the number of DSNs in the proposed scheme increases more gradually compared to other schemes. Coupled with its proficient path planning strategy, this results in the most favorable rate of increase in DSN delay. In contrast, the delay of non-DSNs in the proposed scheme grows slightly faster than that of the JERDC and DGCS schemes. This phenomenon can be explained by the fact that the JERDC and DGCS schemes utilize multiple MCs, whereas the non-DSNs in the proposed scheme rely solely on a single MCO for charging. Despite this, the growth rate remains within an acceptable range. In comparison, the SPSS and CIBA-MDSA schemes witness a relatively rapid increase in delay. This is mainly due to the significantly faster growth of the number of anchors in these schemes, compounded by the inferior performance of their path planning algorithms. As the region size continues to expand, it can be reasonably anticipated that the DSN delay of the proposed scheme will maintain its superiority over other schemes. Similarly, the JERDC and DGCS schemes will continue to outperform the non-DSN schemes in terms of delay. Conversely, the performance of the SPSS scheme and the CIBA-MDSA scheme will progressively deteriorate.

Figure 4b shows that as the area size increases, the path length of the MC indeed exhibits an upward trend. However, it is notable that the charging efficiencies of all schemes, except for the DGCS scheme, demonstrate an increasing tendency. This phenomenon can be attributed to the fact that as the network area expands, the waiting time of nodes also increases. Consequently, the MC is required to remain at the charging position for a longer duration, thereby resulting in an increase in the proportion of energy utilized by the MC for charging and ultimately enhancing the charging efficiency. In contrast, the DGCS scheme exhibits a fluctuating charging efficiency. This is primarily due to its utilization of multiple MCs. As the area increases, the increase in the charging time per MC is not substantial, leading to the observed fluctuations in charging efficiency. The proposed scheme exhibits superior charging efficiency compared to several other schemes. This superiority can be attributed to two key factors. Firstly, the proposed scheme features a relatively shorter path length for the MC. Secondly, it employs full charging, which enables the full utilization of the MC's energy. Among the other schemes, the SPSS scheme and the CIBA-MDSA scheme, although they also adopt full charging, suffer from lower charging efficiencies due to the longer paths traversed by their MCs. The DGCS scheme demonstrates the lowest charging efficiency. This is because it deploys multiple MCs, and each MC's energy used for charging is relatively low, thus resulting in inefficiency. The JERDC scheme is the least efficient as it employs partial charging, which leads to the underutilization of the MC's energy. Regarding the rate of increase in charging efficiency, the proposed scheme continues to experience an increase. The SPSS scheme and the JERDC scheme display a relatively slower rate of increase. The DGCS scheme exhibits fluctuations. The CIBA-MDSA scheme initially increases at a rate similar to that of the proposed scheme. However, in experiments conducted in larger regions, its rate of increase in charging efficiency is bound to slow down due to the inferior performance of its path optimization component. In conclusion, as the region size continues to expand, the proposed scheme maintains its superiority in terms of charging efficiency over several other schemes.

Figure 4c illustrates that as the network expands, the residual energy of the nodes tends to decrease. This can be primarily attributed to the elongation of the MC path length, which leads to a longer node charging delay. Consequently, the nodes consume more energy during the simulation process, leading to a reduction in their residual energy at the end. Notably, the nodes in the proposed scheme maintain a consistently high level of residual energy. This advantageous outcome can be ascribed to the independent charging mechanisms designed specifically for DSNs and non-DSNs in our proposed scheme. These mechanisms effectively balance the energy consumption between the two types of nodes, thereby ensuring a relatively stable energy reserve. The SPSS, CIBA-MDSA, and DGCS schemes also exhibit a relatively high level of residual energy. This is mainly due to their use of the full charging approach, which enables the nodes to receive sufficient energy replenishment. In contrast, the JERDC scheme demonstrates the lowest residual energy among all the schemes. The root cause of this lies in its utilization of the partial charging mechanism, which fails to fully meet the energy requirements of the nodes. When considering the rate of decrease in residual energy, the JERDC scheme exhibits the most significant decline. This is an inevitable consequence of its partial charging method. In contrast, the remaining three schemes, namely the proposed scheme, the SPSS scheme, and the CIBA-MDSA scheme, display a similar rate of decrease. This similarity can be explained by their shared use of the full charging approach. In summary, as the area size continues to increase, the proposed scheme, along with the SPSS, CIBA-MDSA, and DGCS schemes, will maintain higher energy levels. In contrast, the residual energy of the JERDC scheme will remain lower compared to the other four schemes.

5.2.2. Varying the Number of Nodes

In Figure 5, we set the number of nodes to 300, 350, 400, 450, and 500, the size of simulation region to 400 m, the data sense rate of nodes to 128 bit/s, and the number of nodes as the horizontal coordinates of the figures.

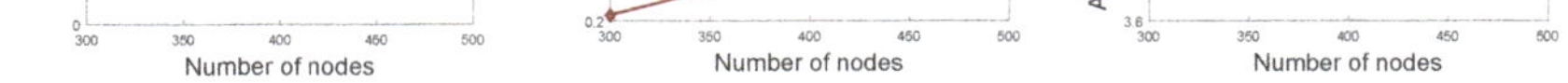

(a) (b) (c)

Figure 5. Impact of the number of nodes. Where (**a**) depicts the simulation results of average delay, (**b**) depicts the simulation results of charging efficiency and (**c**) shows the simulation results of nodes' average residual energy.

Figure 5a clearly indicates that as the number of nodes increases within the range from 300 to 500, a consistent upward trend in delay is observed across all scenarios. This can be primarily attributed to the fact that an increase in the number of nodes leads to a corresponding growth in the data collected by the MC in all scenarios. Concurrently, the energy consumption of the DSNs also rises. These factors jointly result in an inevitable increase in both the charging time and the data reception time, thereby giving rise to the observed increase in delay. In the proposed scheme, it is notable that the delay of the DSNs remains consistently lower than that of the other schemes. This favorable outcome can be ascribed to the utilization of communication radius clustering in the proposed scheme.

This clustering method effectively reduces the number of anchors, thus contributing to the delay reduction. Although the delay of the non-DSNs is slightly higher than that of the JERDC and DGCS schemes, it should be noted that both the JERDC and DGCS schemes employ multiple MCs, whereas the proposed scheme utilizes only a single MCO to charge the non-DSNs. Moreover, considering that the DSN delay in the proposed scheme is lower than that of the JERDC and DGCS schemes, this slight increase in non-DSN delay can be regarded as an acceptable trade-off. In contrast, the delays of the SPSS and CIBA-MDSA schemes are significantly higher than those of the other three schemes. This is primarily because these programs fail to take into account the impact of delay during the path planning process. When analyzing the growth rate of delay with respect to the increase in the number of nodes, it is found that the delay of the DSNs in the proposed scheme exhibits the lowest growth rate. Meanwhile, the growth rate of the non-DSNs is slightly higher than that of the JERDC and DGCS schemes. The SPSS scheme continues to experience a relatively high growth rate. For the CIBA-MDSA scheme, although the delay decreases when the number of nodes reaches 500, its inferior path planning algorithm implies that as the number of nodes continues to increase further, the delay is bound to increase. In conclusion, as the number of nodes continues to grow, the DSNs in the proposed scheme will maintain lower delay, and the non-DSN delay will remain lower than in the SPSS and CIBA-MDSA schemes.

Figure 5b reveals that as the number of nodes increases, the charging efficiencies of these schemes generally display an upward trend. This can be primarily ascribed to the augmented energy consumption of the DSNs, which prompts the MC to allocate more energy for node charging. When the number of nodes is subject to variation, the charging efficiency of the proposed scheme consistently outperforms that of several other schemes. This superiority can be attributed to the shorter path length and the full charging mechanism implemented in the proposed scheme. Although the SPSS, CIBA-MDSA, and DGCS schemes also adopt the full charging mechanism, their charging efficiencies remain lower than that of the proposed scheme due to the longer travel distances of the MC. The JERDC scheme exhibits the lowest charging efficiency on account of its partial charging mechanism. Regarding the rate of increase in charging efficiency, the proposed algorithm experiences a more rapid growth as the number of nodes rises. The DGCS, SPSS, and JERDC schemes follow with the next highest rates of increase. In contrast, the CIBA-MDSA scheme demonstrates the lowest rate of increase in charging efficiency, which can be attributed to the suboptimal performance of its path planning algorithm. Consequently, as the number of nodes continues to expand, the proposed algorithm is expected to maintain the highest charging efficiency among these schemes.

Figure 5c demonstrates that a decreasing tendency in node residual energy is exhibited by all schemes, with the exception of the JERDC scheme. The reason for this anomaly in the JERDC scheme lies in its employment of a partial charging mechanism. When the number of nodes increases, the DSNs in the JERDC scheme consume more energy. Concurrently, the MC may spend a longer time in the vicinity of these nodes, and the non-DSNs receive more energy, thereby resulting in an overall increase in node energy. However, as the number of nodes gradually increases, the charging delay of the nodes also rises. This delay can potentially lead to a reduction in the residual energy of the nodes. As a consequence, the average residual energy of the nodes in the JERDC method fluctuates within a specific range. For the remaining schemes, the higher energy consumption of DSNs and the need for MCs to collect more data necessitate that the nodes require more time to replenish their charge. This ultimately leads to a decrease in the average residual energy of the nodes. In contrast, the proposed scheme yields a relatively higher residual energy of the nodes. This is attributable to the utilization of distinct charging mechanisms for DSNs and non-DSNs.When the number of nodes is on the rise, the proposed scheme and the DGCS scheme exhibit the slowest decreasing trends. The SPSS and CIBA-MDSA schemes display a slightly higher decreasing trend. The JERDC scheme, due to its partial charging mechanism, maintains the lowest and most fluctuating level of node energy. In conclusion, as the number of nodes continues to increase, the node residual energy of the proposed algorithm will consistently remain higher than that of several other schemes.

5.2.3. Varying the Amount of Data Sense Rate of Nodes

In Figure 6, we set the data sense rate of nodes to 32 bit/s, 64 bit/s, 96 bit/s, 128 bit/s, and 160 bit/s, the number of nodes to 400, the size of simulation region to 400 m, and the data sense rate of the nodes as the horizontal coordinates of the figures.

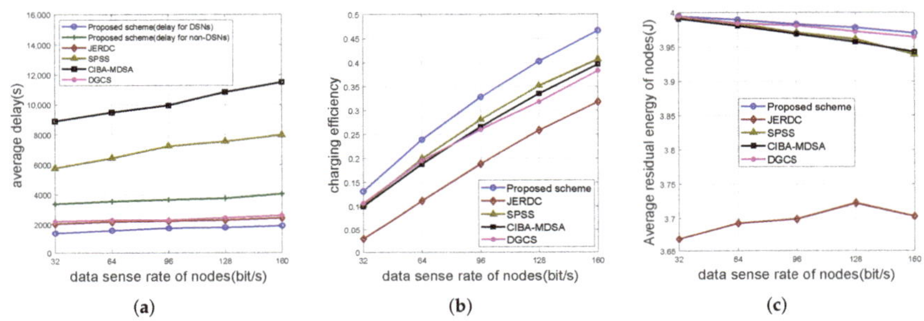

Figure 6. Impact of the number of nodes. Where (**a**) depicts the simulation results of average delay, (**b**) depicts the simulation results of charging efficiency and (**c**) shows the simulation results of nodes' average residual energy.

As depicted in Figure 6a, when the data sensing rate of the node is altered within the range from 32 bit/s to 160 bit/s, an increasing tendency in the delay of all scenarios is observed. This phenomenon is mainly due to the elevation of the node's data sensing rate, which consequentially gives rise to an augmentation in energy consumption and the volume of data cached by the node. Subsequently, the time expended by the MC for charging the nodes and collecting data is prolonged, thereby culminating in an increase in delay. Furthermore, in the proposed scheme, the employment of the minimum number of anchors effectively curtails the path length of the MCDs. This reduction, in turn, mitigates the charging delay for DSNs and the data collection delay of the network. In the JERDC scheme, the strategy of deploying two MCs traveling in opposite directions manifests a marginal reduction in delay when contrasted with the approach of utilizing only a single MCO for charging non-DSNs. The DGCS scheme exhibits lower delay in comparison to non-DSNs due to the utilization of a greater number of MCs. Although the JERDC and DGCS schemes display slightly lower delay relative to non-DSNs, their delay remains higher than that of DSNs. This implies that the data collection delay of the network in these schemes exceeds that of the proposed algorithm. In contrast, the deficiencies in the path planning algorithms of the SPSS and CIBA-MDSA schemes precipitate significantly elevated delays. Regarding the rate of increase in delay, the proposed algorithm, along with the delays of DSNs and non-DSNs in it, as well as those of the JERDC and DGCS schemes, exhibit a relatively stable and gradual increase. In contrast, the SPSS and CIBA-MDSA schemes experience a more pronounced rate of increase in delay. Consequently, the proposed scheme also demonstrates superior performance even when the data sensing rate continues to escalate.

In Figure 6b, as the data sensing rate of the node increases, its energy consumption rises proportionally. Consequently, the MC is required to supply a greater amount of charge to the node. This leads to an upward trend in the charging efficiency of each scheme. The proposed algorithm demonstrates a higher charging efficiency. This is primarily attributed to its utilization of full charging and a shorter path traversed by the MC. Although the SPSS, CIBA-MDSA, and DGCS schemes also adopt full charging, their charging efficiencies are lower than that of the proposed scheme. This is due to the suboptimal performance of their path planning algorithms. In contrast, the JERDC scheme employs partial charging, which results in the lowest charging efficiency among all the schemes. Regarding the rate of increase in charging efficiency, these algorithms exhibit relatively similar trends. Therefore, as the node sensing rate continues to escalate, the proposed algorithm continues to display the highest charging efficiency.

Figure 6c illustrates a decreasing trend in the residual energy of nodes in the proposed SPSS, CIBA-MDSA, and DGCS schemes. This can be primarily attributed to the fact that the energy consumption of the node is directly proportional to the data sensing rate. As the node's energy consumption increases, the charging time of the MC increases, thereby resulting in a longer charging delay. This delay, in turn, leads to a reduction in the node's residual energy. In contrast, the JERDC scheme, which employs a partial charging mechanism, experiences a different scenario. In this case, the energy consumption of the DSNs grows at a faster rate than that of the non-DSNs. As a consequence, the MC remains at the anchor point for a longer duration, enabling it to supply more power to the node. This ultimately leads to an increase in the node's residual energy. However, when the data sensing rate of the node reaches 160 bits/s, the node's energy consumption becomes excessively high, potentially causing a decrease in the residual energy of the node. It is particularly remarkable that the proposed algorithm exhibits the maximum residual energy among the nodes. This is due to the innovative separate charging mechanisms for DSNs and non-DSNs. In the DGCS scheme, although it utilizes more MCs and full charging, its nodes' residual energy is slightly lower than that of the proposed algorithm. The SPSS and CIBA-MDSA schemes, despite also employing full charging, possess lower residual energy levels in their nodes compared to the DGCS scheme. This is primarily because of the inferior performance of their path planning methods. On the other hand, the JERDC scheme demonstrates the least residual energy in its nodes due to the use of partial charging. As the node sensing rate continues to increase, the node energy levels in the proposed scheme and the DGCS scheme decreases at a similar rate. In contrast, the node energy levels in the SPSS and CIBA-MDSA schemes decreases at a faster pace. Meanwhile, the node energy level in the JERDC scheme remains relatively low and fluctuates within a certain range due to the partial charging mechanism. In conclusion, the proposed scheme is capable of maintaining a higher level of node residual energy even as the node sensing rate continues to rise.

5.2.4. The Cost of the Schemes

As shown from Table 4, CIBA-MDSA uses the fewest MCs in the simulation environment of this paper, which is only one. This also explains why its network delay is much higher than that of several other schemes. The proposed scheme, the JERDC scheme, and the SPSS scheme use the same number of MCs—two. The proposed scheme has more significant advantages in terms of network delay, charging efficiency, and node residual energy due to the innovative mechanism of using two types of MCs. The DGCS scheme uses the highest number of MCs—three—and thus its performance in terms of network delay and node residual energy is superior. The proposed scheme uses fewer MCs and has a lower cost as compared to DGCS. Moreover, the MCO in the proposed scheme does not need to carry a data collector, making its cost slightly lower than that of the JERDC and SPSS schemes. The CIBA-MDSA scheme has the worst network performance, though it uses only one MC and has the lowest cost. Therefore, the proposed scheme balances the network's performance and cost.

Table 4. The number of MCs used in different schemes.

Schemes	No. of MCs in Var. Size	No. of MCs in Var. Nodes	No. of MCs in Var. Rate
Proposed scheme	2	2	2
JERDC	2	2	2
SPSS	2	2	2
CIBA-MDSA	1	1	1
DGCS	3	3	3

6. Conclusions and Future Work

This paper proposes a joint optimization scheme for energy replenishment and data collection. The scheme first selects DSNs and non-DSNs and then innovatively employs two different MCs (MCD and MCO) to serve these two types of nodes, which reduces the workload and travel distance of the MCs by combining the capabilities of two different MC types. The scheme's performance demonstrates its potential for optimizing the charging and data transmission strategies, thereby enhancing the overall efficiency of the wireless rechargeable sensor network. In the future, we will focus on the following points for further research:

1. Impacts of real terrain, obstacles, and node failures: in the real world, rolling terrain, obstacles, and the possibility of node failures can have a significant impact on the network. In the future, we will consider these effects in order to further connect the scheme to the real world.
2. Proposed scheme in large-scale networks: In large-scale networks, there is a need to increase the number of MCDs and MCOs to serve the nodes in time and ensure the performance of the network. In larger and more extreme scale networks, there will be node unreachability. We need to optimize the location of the base station so that the MC covers all the nodes in order that the nodes can be served by the MC. In sparse networks, the nodes will be clustered individually and only the MCD is needed in the network without the MCO. How to schedule the MCD for this scenario is another one of our future research directions.
3. Clustering algorithm in the proposed scheme: The clustering algorithm is the core of our proposed scheme; we cluster the nodes based on their geographical location using a density-based approach. In the future, we will consider other factors of the nodes and assign weights to the nodes to improve the performance of the clustering algorithm.
4. Node mobility: We have considered static networks in order to simplify the model. In future work, we will consider dynamic networks where nodes are movable to further optimize the algorithm.

Author Contributions: Conceptualization, Y.L. and F.L.; methodology, Y.L. and F.L.; software, Y.L. and T.S.; validation, Y.L. and W.G.; formal analysis, Y.L.; investigation, W.G. and T.S.; resources, W.G.; data curation, Y.L. and F.L.; writing—original draft preparation, Y.L.; writing—review and editing, Y.L., T.S. and F.L.; visualization, Y.L.; supervision, F.L. All authors have read and agreed to the published version of the manuscript.

Funding: This work is supported by the Sichuan Science and Technology Program (grant no. 2022YFQ0035).

Institutional Review Board Statement: Not applicable.

Informed Consent Statement: Not applicable.

Data Availability Statement: Data are contained within the article.

Conflicts of Interest: The authors declare no conflicts of interest.

Abbreviations

The following abbreviations are used in this manuscript:

MC	Mobile charger
MCD	Mobile charger and data collectors
MCO	Mobile charger only
DSN	Data storage node
WRSN	Wireless rechargeable sensor network
BS	Base station

References

1. Gupta, S.; Akhtar, M.A.K. A review of wireless charging in wsn. In *Trends in Wireless Communication and Information Security. Proceedings of EWCIS 2020*; Springer: Singapore, 2021; pp. 261–271.
2. Kaswan, A.; Jana, P.K.; Das, S.K. A Survey on Mobile Charging Techniques in Wireless Rechargeable Sensor Networks. *IEEE Commun. Surv. Tutor.* **2022**, *24*, 1750–1779. [CrossRef]
3. Huan, X.; Chen, W.; Wang, T.; Hu, H.; Zheng, Y. A One-Way Time Synchronization Scheme for Practical Energy-Efficient LoRa Network Based on Reverse Asymmetric Framework. *IEEE Trans. Commun.* **2021**, *71*, 6468–6481. [CrossRef]
4. Huan, X.; He, H.; Wang, T.; Wu, Q.; Hu, H. A Timestamp-Free Time Synchronization Scheme Based on Reverse Asymmetric Framework for Practical Resource-Constrained Wireless Sensor Networks. *IEEE Trans. Commun.* **2021**, *70*, 6109–6121. [CrossRef]
5. Kandris, D.; Nakas, C.; Vomvas, D.; Koulouras, G. Applications of Wireless Sensor Networks: An Up-to-Date Survey. *Appl. Syst. Innov.* **2020**, *3*, 14. [CrossRef]
6. Huda, S.M.A.; Arafat, M.Y.; Moh, S. Wireless power transfer in wirelessly powered sensor networks: A review of recent progress *Sensors* **2022**, *22*, 2952. [CrossRef] [PubMed]
7. Hong, Y.; Yang, Y.; Luo, C.; Li, D.; Lu, Y.; Chen, Z. Spatiotemporal Optimization for Charging Scheduling in Wireless Rechargeable Sensor Networks. *IEEE Internet Things J.* **2024**, *11*, 3056–3067. [CrossRef]
8. Huang, S.; Sha, C.; Zhu, X.; Wang, J.; Wang, R. Charging Scheduling Method for Wireless Rechargeable Sensor Networks Based on Energy Consumption Rate Prediction for Nodes. *Sensors* **2024**, *24*, 5931. [CrossRef]
9. Xue, H.; Chen, H.; Ni, Z.; Liu, X.; Xia, F. Towards Maximizing Coverage of Targets for WRSNs by Multiple Chargers Scheduling *IEEE Trans. Mob. Comput.* **2024**, *23*, 9959–9970. [CrossRef]
10. Jiang, B.; Wu, M.; Liang, B. Safety Evaluation Method of Tunnel Construction System in Rechargeable Wireless Sensor Networks *IEEE Sens. J.* **2023**, *23*, 20856–20864. [CrossRef]
11. Han, G.; Yang, X.; Liu, L.; Zhang, W. A Joint Energy Replenishment and Data Collection Algorithm in Wireless Rechargeable Sensor Networks. *IEEE Internet Things J.* **2018**, *5*, 2596–2604. [CrossRef]
12. Boukerche, A.; Wu, Q.; Sun, P. A Novel Joint Optimization Method Based on Mobile Data Collection for Wireless Rechargeable Sensor Networks. *IEEE Trans. Green Commun. Netw.* **2018**, *5*, 1610–1622. [CrossRef]
13. Jiao, W.; Tian, M.; Xu, Y. A Combining Strategy of Energy Replenishment and Data Collection in Wireless Sensor Networks. *IEEE Sens. J.* **2022**, *22*, 7411–7426. [CrossRef]
14. Chen, Y.; Jiao, W.; Yu, W. The Combined Strategy of Energy Replenishment and Data Collection in Heterogenous Wireless Rechargeable Sensor Networks. *IEEE Syst. J.* **2023**, *17*, 4267–4278. [CrossRef]
15. Li, J.; Sun, G.; Wang, A.; Lei, M.; Liang, S.; Kang, H.; Liu, Y. A many-objective optimization charging scheme for wireless rechargeable sensor networks via mobile charging vehicles. *Comput. Netw.* **2021**, *215*, 109196. [CrossRef]
16. Han, G.; Guan, H.; Wu, J.; Chan, S.; Shu, L.; Zhang, W. An Uneven Cluster-Based Mobile Charging Algorithm for Wireless Rechargeable Sensor Networks. *IEEE Syst. J.* **2019**, *13*, 3747–3758. [CrossRef]
17. Han, G.; Wu, J.; Wang, H.; Guizani, M.; Ansere, J.A.; Zhang, W. A Multicharger Cooperative Energy Provision Algorithm Based on Density Clustering in the Industrial Internet of Things. *IEEE Internet Things J.* **2019**, *6*, 9165–9174. [CrossRef]
18. Dong, Y.; Li, S.; Bao, G.; Wang, C. An Efficient Combined Charging Strategy for Large-Scale Wireless Rechargeable Sensor Networks. *IEEE Sens. J.* **2020**, *20*, 10306–10315. [CrossRef]
19. Zhu, F.; Lv, X.; Li, G.; Tang, H.; Guo, F. Fuzzy cluster-based multi-node charging strategy in mobile sensor networks. *Ad Hoc Netw.* **2024**, *156*, 103439. [CrossRef]
20. Lyu, Z.; Wei, Z.; Wang, X.; Fan, Y.; Xia, C.; Shi, L. A Periodic Multinode Charging and Data Collection Scheme With Optimal Traveling Path in WRSNs. *IEEE Syst. J.* **2019**, *14*, 3518–3529. [CrossRef]

21. Zhang, Y.; He, S.; Chen, J. Near Optimal Data Gathering in Rechargeable Sensor Networks with a Mobile Sink. *IEEE Trans. Mob. Comput.* **2017**, *16*, 1718–1729. [CrossRef]
22. Lu, Z.; Fan, B.; Cai, J.; Tang, L. J-RCA: A Joint Routing and Charging Algorithm With WCE Assisted Data Gathering in Wireless Rechargeable Sensor Networks. *IEEE Sens. J.* **2021**, *21*, 3888–3899. [CrossRef]
23. Lu, Z.; Fan, B.; Cai, J.; Tang, L. Mobile data gathering and energy harvesting in rechargeable wireless sensor networks. *Inf. Sci.* **2019**, *482*, 189–209. [CrossRef]
24. Nguyen, N.; Liu, B.; Pham, V.; Huang, C. Network Under Limited Mobile Devices: A New Technique for Mobile Charging Scheduling With Multiple Sinks. *IEEE Syst. J.* **2018**, *12*, 2186–2196. [CrossRef]
25. Liu, K.; Peng, J.; He, L.; Pan, J.; Li, S.; Ling, M.; Huang, Z. An Active Mobile Charging and Data Collection Scheme for Clustered Sensor Networks. *IEEE Trans. Veh. Technol.* **2019**, *68*, 5100–5113. [CrossRef]
26. Ijemaru, G.; Ang, L.; Seng, K.P. Optimizing Energy Consumption and Provisioning for Wireless Charging and Data Collection in Large-Scale WRSNs With Mobile Elements. *IEEE Internet Things J.* **2023**, *10*, 17585–17602. [CrossRef]
27. Zhang, Q.; Li, F.; Wang, Y. Mobile Crowd Wireless Charging Toward Rechargeable Sensors for Internet of Things. *IEEE Internet Things J.* **2018**, *5*, 5337–5347. [CrossRef]
28. Nguyen, T.D.; Nguyen, T.; Nguyen, T.; Nguyen, K.; Nguyen, P.L. Joint Optimization of Charging Location and Time for Network Lifetime Extension in WRSNs. *IEEE Trans. Green Commun. Netw.* **2022**, *6*, 1186–1197. [CrossRef]
29. Cheng, Y.Z. Mean shift, mode seeking, and clustering. *IEEE Trans. Pattern Anal. Mach. Intell.* **1995**, *17*, 790–799. [CrossRef]
30. Wang, X.F.; Ziavras, S.G. Parallel LU factorization of sparse matrices on FPGA-based configurable computing engines. *Concurr. Comput.-Pract. Exp.* **2004**, *16*, 319–343. [CrossRef]
31. Yadav, C.B.K.; Dash, D. An energy efficient periodic data gathering and charging schedule using mvs in wireless rechargeable sensor networks. *Computing* **2023**, *105*, 2563–2593. [CrossRef]
32. Liu, B.; Nguyen, N.; Pham, V.; Lin, Y. Novel methods for energy charging and data collection in wireless rechargeable sensor networks. *J. Int. J. Commun. Syst.* **2017**, *30*, e3050. [CrossRef]
33. Gao, Z.; Liu, C.; Chen, Y. Scheduling of erd-assisted charging of a wrsn using a directional mobile charger. *IEEE Trans. Mob. Comput.* **2024**, *23*, 6681–6696. [CrossRef]
34. Dande, B.; Chang, C.Y.; Wu, S.J.; Roy, D.S. Wlars: Workload-aware recharge scheduling mechanism for improving surveillance quality in wireless rechargeable sensor networks. *IEEE Sens. J.* **2023**, *23*, 12237–12250. [CrossRef]
35. Dande, B.; Chang, C.Y.; Kuo, C.H.; Roy, D.S. Rs-stq: Recharge scheduling algorithm for maximizing spatial and temporal data accuracy. *IEEE Sens. J.* **2022**, *22*, 23565–23580. [CrossRef]
36. Deng, T.; Tang, S.; Chen, Y.; Lin, F. A Hybrid Charging Scheme for Minimizing the Number of Energy-Exhausted Nodes in Wireless Rechargeable Sensor Networks. *IEEE Sens. J.* **2024**, *24*, 17169–17182. [CrossRef]
37. Jain, D.; Shukla, P.K.; Varma, S. Energy efficient architecture for mitigating the hot-spot problem in wireless sensor networks. *J. Ambient Intell. Humaniz. Comput.* **2023**, *14*, 10587–10604. [CrossRef]

micromachines

MDPI

Article

Effects of Aerodynamic Parameters on Performance of Galloping Piezoelectric Energy Harvester Based on Cross-Sectional Shape Evolutionary Approach

Xiaokang Yang *, Bingke Xu, Zhendong Shang, Junying Tian, Haichao Cai and Xiangyi Hu

School of Mechatronics Engineering, Henan University of Science and Technology, Luoyang 471002, China; xbk1026@163.com (B.X.); jdszd@haust.edu.cn (Z.S.); tjy@haust.edu.cn (J.T.); chc1226@haust.edu.cn (H.C.); hxy230626@haust.edu.cn (X.H.)

* Correspondence: yangxiaokang@haust.edu.cn

Abstract: This study explores the potential effects of the aerodynamic parameters on the performance of the galloping piezoelectric energy harvester. By considering the geometric configurations, a bluff body cross-sectional shape evolution approach is proposed using Boolean operations on the polygons and forty-eight different cross-sectional shapes with the protruding and depressed features are considered. Computational fluid dynamics is employed to perform a time-varying simulation of the aerodynamic characteristics. The effects of the aerodynamic parameters on performance are investigated computationally using a distributed parameter electromechanical coupling model. The critical wind speed, maximum output power, and the slope of the power versus wind speed curve are introduced as the performance evaluation parameters. The results show that the rear-side protruding feature and the top-side and bottom-side depressed feature have significant potential to enhance the performance. Furthermore, a symmetrical structure of the cross-sectional shape in the downstream direction should be prioritized over asymmetric designs.

Keywords: energy harvesting; piezoelectricity; galloping; aerodynamic parameter

1. Introduction

Micro-energy devices that convert ambient energy into electrical energy have been developed in recent years [1–3]. They can provide a continuous and stable energy supply for low-power electronic devices that are far from the power grid and can extend their service lives [4]. Piezoelectric energy harvesters [5,6], electromagnetic energy harvesters [7,8], triboelectric nanogenerators [9,10], and electrostatic energy generators [11,12] are the main types of micro-energy devices. Piezoelectric energy harvesters based on wind-induced vibration have been extensively researched due to the widespread availability of environmental wind energy, which is developed on a large scale [13]. Additionally, piezoelectric materials have high voltage output and are easily compatible with microelectromechanical systems [14]. Piezoelectric energy harvesters based on wind-induced vibration have vast potential for applications in large-span regional environmental parameter monitoring applications.

Structures in contact with airflow, whether natural or human-made, are inevitably subject to wind-induced vibration, which mainly includes galloping, vortex-induced vibration and buffeting, etc. [15] Galloping is a typical aerodynamic instability phenomenon with large-amplitude vibration and self-excitation properties [16]. This is beneficial when using the piezoelectric transducer because the output voltage is related to the amplitude of these oscillations [17]. The necessary condition for galloping is that the slope of the lift force coefficient is more negative than the drag force coefficient when the angle of attack of incoming flow is 0°. Structures with non-circular cross-sectional shapes are likely to experience galloping. Ice-covered wires, high-rise buildings, lamp poles, chimneys, and towers are typical structural types. Under the action of airflow, the total damping of the elastic system consists of linear damping and nonlinear damping. The former is composed of structural damping and linear aerodynamic negative damping, and the latter is nonlinear aerodynamic negative damping. When the wind speed exceeds a certain threshold (critical wind speed), the linear aerodynamic negative damping causes the total damping of the system to be negative, and the bluff body produces a single-degree-of-freedom divergent vibration with crosswind bending, while the nonlinear aerodynamic negative damping causes it to produce limited motion.

The common structural characteristics of the galloping-based piezoelectric energy harvester (GPEH) are a bluff body and a piezoelectric composite beam [13]. The bluff body drives or its galloping wake induces the vibration of the piezoelectric composite beam, and an electrical output is obtained on the load. The purpose of using mathematical models and experiments to analyze the effects of parameters on performance is to obtain the best structural design. The parameters of the GPEH mainly include aerodynamic, structural, motion, and electrical parameters. The galloping aerodynamic coefficient, which is obtained based on experiments or simulation processes, is mainly determined by factors such as cross-sectional shape, turbulence intensity, and Reynolds number. It is usually expressed as a function of the aerodynamic lift and drag coefficients and the angle of attack of incoming flow. The structural, motion, and electrical parameters mainly include the dimensional characteristics of the bluff body and piezoelectric composite beam, equivalent mass, natural frequency, mechanical and electrical damping ratio, electromechanical coupling coefficient, capacitance, and optimized load, etc. The effects of the structural, motion, and electrical parameters on performance can be analyzed adequately using the model; however, this is not applicable to the aerodynamic parameters, which are mainly determined by the cross-sectional shape of the GPEH's bluff body. Manually changing the aerodynamic parameters will result in an unknown cross-sectional shape.

A reliable and accurate mathematical model is a prerequisite for the development of an optimal GPEH. The three commonly used types of mathematical models include the single-degree-of-freedom lumped parameter model, the approximated distributed parameter model based on Rayleigh–Ritz discretization, and the distributed parameter model based on Euler–Bernoulli beam theory [18]. The Gauss law and quasi-steady hypothesis are used to relate the mechanical and electrical variables and to evaluate the galloping force, respectively. The coupled nonlinear electroaeroelastic distributed-parameter model based on Euler–Bernoulli beam theory was developed by Abdelkefi et al. [19] in 2013, and it was validated using the previous experimental results of Sirohi and Mahadik [20]. The effects of the load resistance and wind speed on the performance of the GPEH have been studied, and the results showed that the onset(critical) speed is strongly affected by the electrical load resistance. Zhao et al. [21] developed a comparison study on the performance of the modeling methods, including the single-degree-of-freedom lumped parameter model and the single mode and multimode Euler–Bernoulli distributed parameter models. The influence of the load resistance, wind exposure area, mass of the bluff body, and length of the piezoelectric sheets on the cut-in(critical) wind speed, as well as the output power level, were fully investigated. It was demonstrated that all the considered models could accurately predict the performance of the harvester.

The research on the effects of aerodynamic characteristics on the performance of GPEHs based on the different cross-sectional shapes is well developed and includes studies of shapes that are square [22], rectangular [23], triangular [24,25], D-shaped [22], elliptical [26,27], V-shaped [28], W-shaped [29], Y-shaped [30], fork-shaped [31], sinusoidal wavy protuberances on square [32], circular with different rod-shaped attachments [33], and rectangular, triangular, and elliptical metasurface protrusions [34]. Their results confirmed the superiority of the square cross-sectional shape compared to the rectangular, triangular, and D-shaped; sinusoidal wavy protuberances on a square bluff body could be used as a passive control to tune the critical galloping velocity; the rear protrusions of rectangular, triangular, and elliptical metasurfaces can enhance the galloping response; and the power generated by the square bluff body with a specific ratio of V-shaped groove depths is much higher than that of the square bluff body at the same wind speed. A common characteristic of these studies is that the irregular changes in cross-sectional shapes were used; consequently, the conclusions were non-universal, which makes it difficult to design a structure guided by specific performance requirements.

In this study, an evolutionary approach to the bluff body cross-sectional shape of the GPEH is proposed, with the aim of systematically investigating the potential effects of aerodynamic parameters on performance; furthermore, the protruding and depressed features around the square bluff body are considered separately. The model, which was proposed in our previous work, is validated in Section 2 by the experimental results of a prototype with a square cross-sectional shape. In Section 3, computational fluid dynamics is employed to perform the time-varying simulation of aerodynamic characteristics for forty-eight bluff bodies with different cross-sectional shapes. In Section 4, the effects of aerodynamic parameters on performance are analyzed using the model. A summary and the conclusions are presented in Section 5.

2. Mathematical Formulation of GPEH

The GPEH comprises a thin piezoelectric cantilever beam rigidly attached at the free end to a bluff body with different cross-sectional shapes [17]. A distributed parameter electromechanical coupling model of a piezoelectric energy harvester based on the interaction between vortex-induced vibration and galloping has been proposed and verified [35]. The distributed parameter model of the GPEH can be obtained under non short circuit conditions and by ignoring the aerodynamic force of vortex-induced vibration [36], and the first-order model can be expressed as follows:

$$\ddot{Y}(t) + 2\omega\xi\dot{Y}(t) + \omega^2 Y(t) + \Theta V(t) = \frac{1}{2}\rho u^2 LD\left[\sum_{i=1}^{N} A_i\left(\frac{\dot{Y}(t)}{u}\right)^i\right], \quad (1)$$

$$\frac{V(t)}{R} + C_p\dot{V}(t) = \Theta\dot{Y}(t), \quad (2)$$

where ω, ξ, and Θ represent the undamped natural frequency, mechanical damping ratio, and piezoelectric coupling term, respectively; A_i represents the polynomial coefficients of the galloping aerodynamic force coefficient, L and D are the height and length of the bluff body; V represents the voltage across the load resistor R; and C_p, u, and ρ represent the total capacitance and wind velocity, respectively.

The time marching using ODE45 is used to obtain the numerical solutions of the displacement or electrical responses, and the flow chart of the simulation process is shown in Figure 1. Prior to this, the accuracy of the initial and convergence conditions must be validated. A slight displacement of the beam should be established as an initial condition for galloping. The convergence condition necessitates that the amplitude error of the aerodynamic coefficient or displacement response of the bluff body between two adjacent time steps must be less than 10^{-5}, or until the calculation time reaches its maximum value. An updated initial amplitude should be considered, which means that the initial amplitude of each velocity calculation point is taken to be equal to the stable amplitude of the previous one, because the hysteresis characteristics of the galloping would not be predicted by considering a fixed initial amplitude.

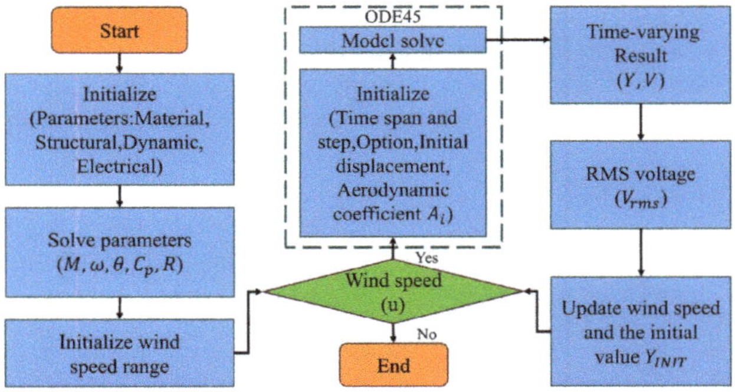

Figure 1. The flow chart of the simulation process.

The distributed parameter model was first validated using the experimental results of the prototype. The prototype was fabricated and tested in a small tunnel, as shown in Figure 2a. The bluff body was constructed from balsa wood with the sides of 4 × 4 × 10 mm and a mass of 0.0291 g. The cantilever was assembled using a 20 μm thick ultraviolet-curing process to attach 200 μm thick polyvinylidene fluoride (PVDF) films to 300 μm thick polyethylene terephthalate (PET) films. According to the model, the numerical first natural frequency, capacitance, and optical load are 97.29 Hz, 132.8 pF, and 12.32 MΩ, respectively. The experimental values are 98.8 Hz, 130.5 pF, and 13 MΩ, as determined using the amplitude–frequency characteristic, impedance analyzer (Microtest-6378, Taipei, China), and load characteristic, respectively, as shown in Figure 2b,c. The numerical results of those parameters agree well with the experimental ones. The numerical equivalent mass and piezoelectric coupling term are 0.03082 g and 1.935×10^{-6} N/V, respectively. The mechanical damping ratio was measured using the logarithmic decrement method [20,37], with values of 1.60–1.87%. The damping is amplitude-dependent [22] and is positively correlated with the amplitude of our experimental results. A variable damping ratio was applied to the calculation process, and a linear fit was used to express the relationship between damping and wind speed, as follows: $\xi = 0.00123u + 0.0044$. The experimental results and numerical results with fixed (1.74%) and variable damping ratios are shown in Figure 3a. The critical wind speed of the experiment is 9.2–9.4 m/s. Once the wind speed exceeds the critical wind speed, the load obtains a larger electrical response. For example, when the wind speeds are 10, 12, and 13.2 m/s, the experimental output powers are 23.1, 26.3, and 27.4 μW, respectively. In the working wind speed range, the experiment power versus wind speed curve is divided into linear and nonlinear regions, and the wind speed ranges are 9.4–11.2 m/s and 11.2–13.2 m/s, respectively. The nonlinear response region may be caused by material and geometric nonlinearity at the relatively high wind speeds. According to previous studies, the geometric nonlinearity of flexible cantilever beam systems under large displacements should be considered for its impact on bluff body motion [38]. This nonlinear strain–deflection relationship will lead to an amplitude reduction trend. Additionally, the piezoelectric material nonlinearity can induce a softening behavior in the system [39]. Therefore, higher-order elastic and electroelastic tensor components in the piezoelectric constitutive equations should be considered during the modeling process. The current model exhibits discrepancies in predicting electrical responses under high wind speeds compared to experimental results, primarily due to the exclusion of nonlinear factors in the modeling framework. With the variable damping ratio, the model accurately predicts the critical wind speed and the electrical response level of the linear region. Since the model does not consider nonlinear factors, the numerical output powers under high wind speed are higher than the experimental values. For example, when the wind speed is 13.2 m/s, the numerical and experimental output powers are 33.7 (fixed damping ratio), 31.1 (variable damping ratio), and 27.4 μW, respectively, with relative errors of 23.0% and 12.4%. In addition, the prototype has a slight electrical output below the critical wind speed, which may be caused by the non-strict symmetry structure of the prototype.

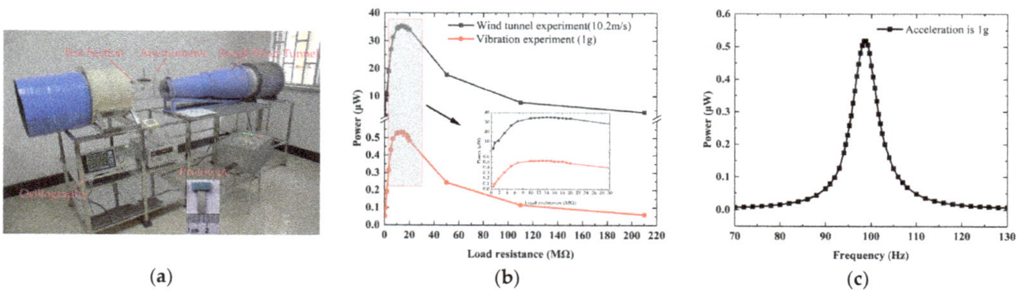

Figure 2. (**a**) The fabricated prototype; (**b**) experimental power versus load; (**c**) experimental power versus frequency.

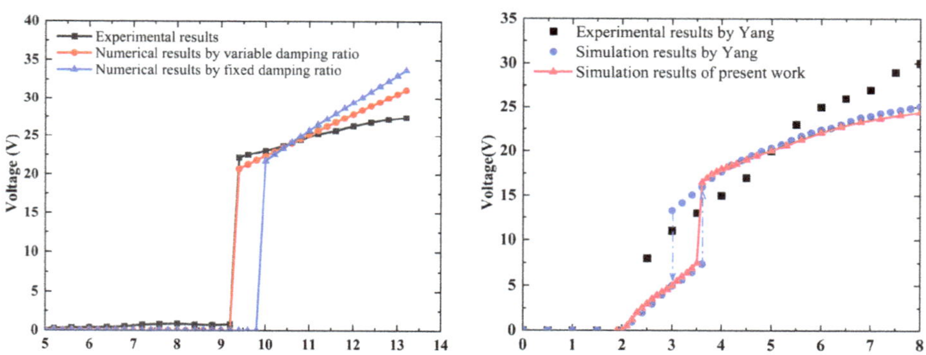

Figure 3. The experimental and numerical results: (**a**) prototype in this work; (**b**) previous study by Yang [22].

In 2013, Yang et al. [22] proposed a prototype of the GPEH with a square cross-sectional shape, and a single-degree-of-freedom lumped parameter model was used for the prediction of the electrical response after the identification of the prototype's parameters. The equivalent mass, natural frequency, damping ratio, piezoelectric coupling term, capacitance, and optimized load are 30.168 g, 6.84 Hz (short circuit) and 6.8 Hz (open circuit), 1.48% (0.5% was used), 0.000373 N/V, 180 nF, and 105 kΩ, respectively. Figure 3b shows a comparison of the predicted results from the current model with the numerical and experimental and simulation data in Yang's study, and the results of the two models are almost the same in terms of critical wind speed and output voltage.

3. Cross-Sectional Shape Evolutionary Approach and Simulation Results

3.1. Evolutionary Approach

GPEHs with different bluff body cross-sectional shapes have been analyzed theoretically and experimentally. Due to its accessibility, the GPEH with a square cross-sectional shape has traditionally been used as the subject of performance comparison. In fact, "a complex cross-sectional shape" is equivalent to a simple geometric pattern, such as a square, triangle, or circle, with variable external contour features. The variable external contour features can also be re-textured by performing Boolean operations on multiple simple geometric patterns. This means that they can be obtained through Boolean operations between multiple simple cross-sectional shapes; for example, a D-shape can be computed using Boolean union regions between a square and a circle. Furthermore, as the size of the outer contour feature gradually decreases, the complex cross-sectional shape will evolve towards a simple one. The evolutionary approach detailing the cross-sectional shapes discussed in this study is shown in Figure 4 and follows the given procedure.

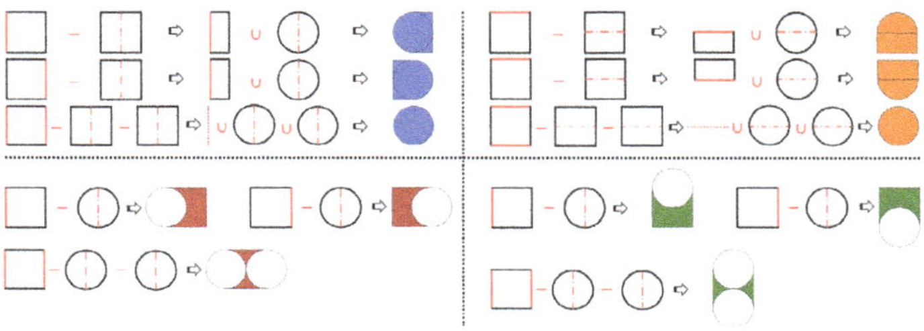

Figure 4. Venn diagram of the bluff body cross-sectional shape evolutionary approach.

(i) Primary and secondary cross-sectional shapes, e.g., a square and a circle, are selected.
(ii) The Boolean difference operation is performed on multiple primary cross-sectional shapes to obtain the auxiliary cross-section shape, e.g., a rectangle, or by selecting the primary cross-sectional shape directly as the auxiliary cross-section shape, e.g., a square.
(iii) The Boolean union or difference operation is performed on the auxiliary cross-sectional shape and multiple secondary cross-sectional shapes to obtain the final cross-sectional shape, e.g., a D-shape, and it evolves towards the primary shape as the number of secondary shapes approaches infinity.
(iv) The final shape is named "$ROUGH^{i-P/D}_{F/R/FR/T/B/TB/FRTB}$", with the superscript and subscript denoting the number and direction of the protruding (P) or depressed (D) features, respectively. For example, $ROUGH^{4-P}_{FRTB}$ means a square cross-sectional shape with the protruding features of four semicircles on the front (F), rear (R), top (T), and bottom (B) sides.

In fact, the evolutionary approach we proposed represents a general method for texturing the bluff body cross-sectional shape of the GPEH and also applies to scenarios such as those in which a square or circle with an equilateral triangle or arched features is used. This approach embodies the logic of the way in which a complex cross-sectional feature evolves towards the simplest and most readily obtainable shape according to a certain pattern. This makes it easier to capture the effect of the cross-sectional shape with the continuous feature changes on aerodynamic characteristics. Consequently, it facilitates the obtainment of the effects of aerodynamic parameters on the behavior, critical wind speed, and electrical response of GPEHs, and thus benefits their structural design. The forty-eight cross-sectional shapes discussed in this study are shown in Figure 5.

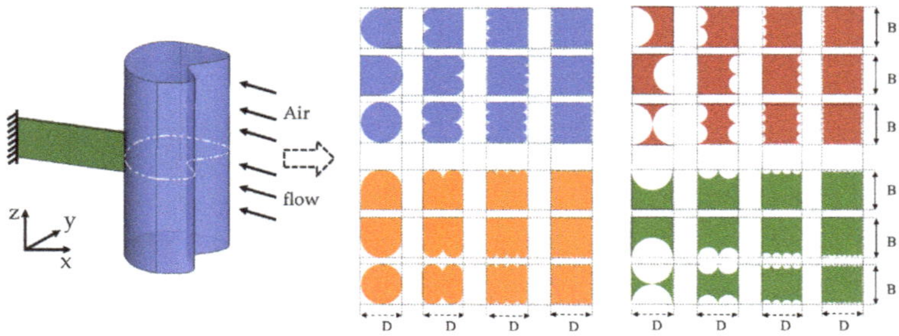

Figure 5. The cross-sectional shapes of the bluff bodies used in this present work.

3.2. Aerodynamic Dynamic Modeling and Validation

To obtain the aerodynamic force on the bluff body, the external flow field is simulated by solving the continuity and the Navier–Stokes equations of incompressible fluid, with the assumption that the external flow field is 2D and unsteady [25,34]. As shown in Figure 6a, the computational domain is rectangular with a size of 70D × 20D, where D is the characteristic dimension of the cross-section of the bluff body. The distances from the center point of the bluff body to the inlet and top wall are 20D and 20D; these distances ensure adequate fluid development and a smaller blocking rate. The settings of the boundary conditions include the velocity inlet, pressure outlet, and symmetric top and bottom walls. A circular mesh refinement area around the bluff body is set, with a diameter of 5D. The height of the first layer of the mesh depends on y+, which needs to be close to 30 for the validity of the standard $k - \varepsilon$ model in the near-wall region. The characteristic length of the bluff body is 0.06 m and the Reynolds number is about 12,322. The time step in the domain-independence study is finally set to 0.0005 s, meeting the requirement of the maximum Courant number to be less than unity.

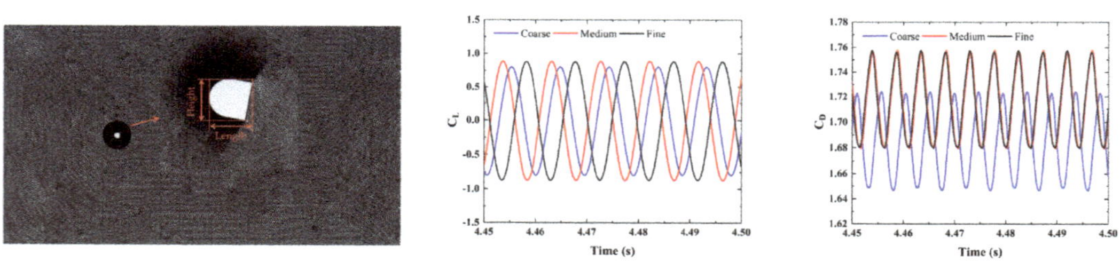

(**a**) (**b**) (**c**)

Figure 6. (**a**) Computational mesh, comparison of results in time domain: (**b**) C_L, (**c**) C_D.

The reference values are used in the computation of the derived physical quantities and non-dimensional coefficients for postprocessing, such as the lift and drag force coefficients. The accuracy of the calculation results is related to the reference value setting. The reference values, which are defined in ANSYS Fluent® 2023 R1, mainly include the area, depth, length, and velocity. To aid understanding of the definition of the reference value, the height variable is introduced in this study. The height and length are the projection dimension of the bluff body in the cross-flow and downstream directions, as shown in Figure 6a, respectively. The depth is the thickness of the bluff body, and its value also needs to be set in 2D simulations. Finally, the area is the projection of the bluff body in the cross-flow direction, which is equal to the product of the height and depth. According to the above definition, the three-dimensional characteristics of the bluff body can be uniquely determined. Three different grid densities are considered to ensure the grid independence. The comparisons of results of the aerodynamic lift and drag coefficients, C_L and C_D, in the time domain are given in Figure 6b,c, when the angle of attack, wind speed, Reynolds number, and turbulence intensity are 0°, 15.3 m/s, 20,000, and 12.5%, respectively. The root mean square (RMS) values of C_L and C_D, given in Table 1, are consistent with the experimental results in Laneville's study [40], and the medium grid number has been selected.

Table 1. Comparison of results of the aerodynamic lift and drag coefficients.

Case	Grid Number	$C_{L(RMS)}$	$C_{D(RMS)}$
Coarse	3.72×10^4	0.566	1.683
Medium	1.03×10^5	0.622 [9.89%]	1.716 [1.90%]
Fine	2.34×10^5	0.624 [0.32%]	1.716 [0.00%]

3.3. Simulation Results of Aerodynamic Characteristics of GPEH

According to the quasi-steady theory proposed by Parkinson [16], the lift and drag coefficients, C_L and C_D, of galloping, in the course of oscillation, are the same at each attack angle α as the values measured at the corresponding steady attack angle α, and the transverse force coefficient C_{Fy} is defined as follows:

$$C_{Fy} = -C_L cos\alpha - C_D sin\alpha = -(C_L + C_D tan\alpha)sec\alpha, \tag{3}$$

In terms of the Den Hartog criterion, a necessary condition for the occurrence of the galloping instability is that the slope of the C_{Fy} versus α curve at α = 0° is positive, and can be expressed as follows:

$$\left.\frac{\partial C_{Fy}}{\partial \alpha}\right|_{\alpha = 0^\circ} = -\left(\frac{\partial C_L}{\partial \alpha} + C_D\right)\Bigg|_{\alpha = 0^\circ} > 0, \tag{4}$$

The numerical results for C_L, C_D, and C_{Fy} of the forty-eight different cross-sectional shapes are shown in Figures 7 and 8, in which the protruding and depressed feature cases are considered. Due to the asymmetric structure in the cross-flow direction, both the positive and negative angles of attack are considered, with a range of −30–30°. The aerodynamic characteristic analysis includes the protruding features on the front and rear sides and the depressed features on the top and bottom sides of the cross-sectional shape.

3.3.1. Protruding and Depressed Features on the Front and Rear Sides

For the protruding feature, as shown in Figure 7a–c, the variation trend of the drag coefficient C_D for the cross-sectional shapes with the front protruding feature is consistent with that of the square one. The values of C_D at all the considered attack angles α are smaller than those of the square, and C_D increases with the number of semicircular features at the same attack angle. This trend is easy to foresee, as the smooth front-side protruding feature causes its C_D to decrease rapidly. Meanwhile, the corresponding values of C_L are all larger than those of the square cross-sectional shape and are even positive. This causes the slope of the aerodynamic coefficient C_{Fy} versus α to be negative at α = 0°, and it also causes C_{Fy} to gradually decreases with the increase in α. Therefore, as shown in Figure 7c, no galloping behavior occurs for cases of $ROUGH_F^{1-P}$, $ROUGH_F^{2-P}$, $ROUGH_F^{4-P}$, $ROUGH_{FR}^{1-P}$, $ROUGH_{FR}^{2-P}$, and $ROUGH_{FR}^{4-P}$, and the GPEH with those cross-sectional shapes will not produce electrical output. It is interesting to note that for the rear-side protruding feature, C_L and C_D have more lower values at the larger attack angles; this results in the peak value and the attack angle corresponding to C_{Fy} = 0 being clearly larger than the square shape.

According to the previous research conducted by Xing et al. [34] and Hu et al. [33], the larger peak value reflects a greater galloping aerodynamic force and displacement response, which is beneficial to the performance improvement of the GPEH.

The depressed feature, as shown in Figure 7d–f, does not have a significant effect on C_L and C_D, and these minor effects are ultimately not reflected in C_{Fy}. It is worth noting that compared to the square shape, the shape with the front-side depressed features has a larger C_D. For example, when $\alpha = 0°$, the C_D values of the shapes of the depressed feature with the semicircular numbers 1, 2, 4, and 8 and the square shape are 1.75, 1.87, 1.70, 1.58, and 1.58, respectively. Within the considered range of α, C_D is between 1.42 and 2.12, and its contribution to C_{Fy} is small. However, the slopes of C_{Fy} versus α at $\alpha = 0°$ are all positive, indicating that all these shapes will experience galloping.

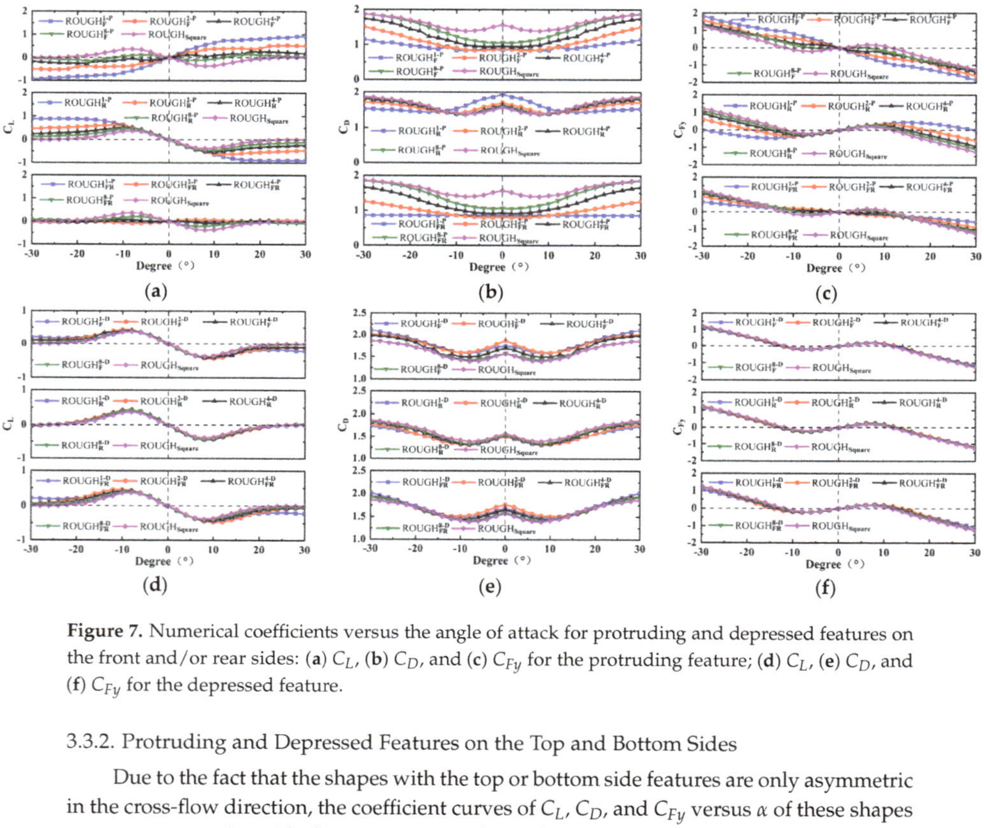

Figure 7. Numerical coefficients versus the angle of attack for protruding and depressed features on the front and/or rear sides: (**a**) C_L, (**b**) C_D, and (**c**) C_{Fy} for the protruding feature; (**d**) C_L, (**e**) C_D, and (**f**) C_{Fy} for the depressed feature.

3.3.2. Protruding and Depressed Features on the Top and Bottom Sides

Due to the fact that the shapes with the top or bottom side features are only asymmetric in the cross-flow direction, the coefficient curves of C_L, C_D, and C_{Fy} versus α of these shapes are not symmetric, with the origin point of coordinate axis in the range $-30° < \alpha < 30°$. Therefore, for those cases, the effects of the protruding and depressed features on C_L, C_D, and C_{Fy} can only be discussed in the range $0° < \alpha < 30°$. For the protruding feature, as shown in Figure 8a–c, the C_L and C_D values are higher and lower, respectively, than the square shape in most cases and are mainly caused by the smooth top or bottom protruding feature cases. This results in the slope of C_{Fy} versus α at $\alpha = 0°$ and the peak value of the C_{Fy} versus α curve are slightly lower than those of the square shape. The α corresponding to $C_{Fy} = 0$ of the square shape is the same as that of the shapes with only top-side or bottom-side features, but larger than that of the shapes with both top-side and bottom-side protruding features. This indicates that the bluff body has smaller galloping oscillations, which is not conducive to the performance improvement of the GPEH with the above cross-sectional shapes. No galloping behavior occurs for cases of $ROUGH_{B}^{1-P}$, $ROUGH_{TB}^{1-P}$, $ROUGH_{TB}^{2-P}$, $ROUGH_{TB}^{4-P}$, and $ROUGH_{TB}^{8-P}$.

An important difference is shown by the depressed feature, as shown in Figure 8d–f. The values of C_L and C_D with the top-side depressed feature are almost the same in $0^\circ < \alpha$ 30°. This is because when α is greater than 0°, the top depressed feature is located on the rear side of the shape and has almost no effect on C_L and C_D. The bottom depressed features have limited effects on C_L and C_D at a smaller α (such as 0–10°), but their effects in a larger α (such as 10–30°) are obvious. According to the results, it can be seen that the degree of influence is positively correlated with the depth of the depressed feature. For example, as shown in Figure 9f, the peak values of C_{Fy} and the α corresponding to $C_{Fy} = 0$ of the depressed feature with the semicircular numbers 1, 2, 4, and 8 and the square shape are 0.88 (10°), 0.41 (8°), 0.27 (6°), 0.24 (6°), 0.20 (6°), and 18–20°, 12–14°, 10–12°, 10–12°, 10–12°, respectively. Therefore, several conclusions can be drawn, as follows:

(i) A symmetrical shape with the depressed feature on the top and bottom sides is necessary.

(ii) The slopes of the aerodynamic coefficient C_{Fy} versus attack angle α curve at $\alpha = 0^\circ$ of the depressed feature shapes are almost the same as that of the square, which leads to an almost consistent critical wind speed.

(iii) The degree of influence is positively correlated with the depth of the depressed feature; therefore, the case of $ROUGH_{UD}^{1-CV}$ has a larger galloping displacement response, and the GPEH with this cross-sectional shape has a much higher electrical output.

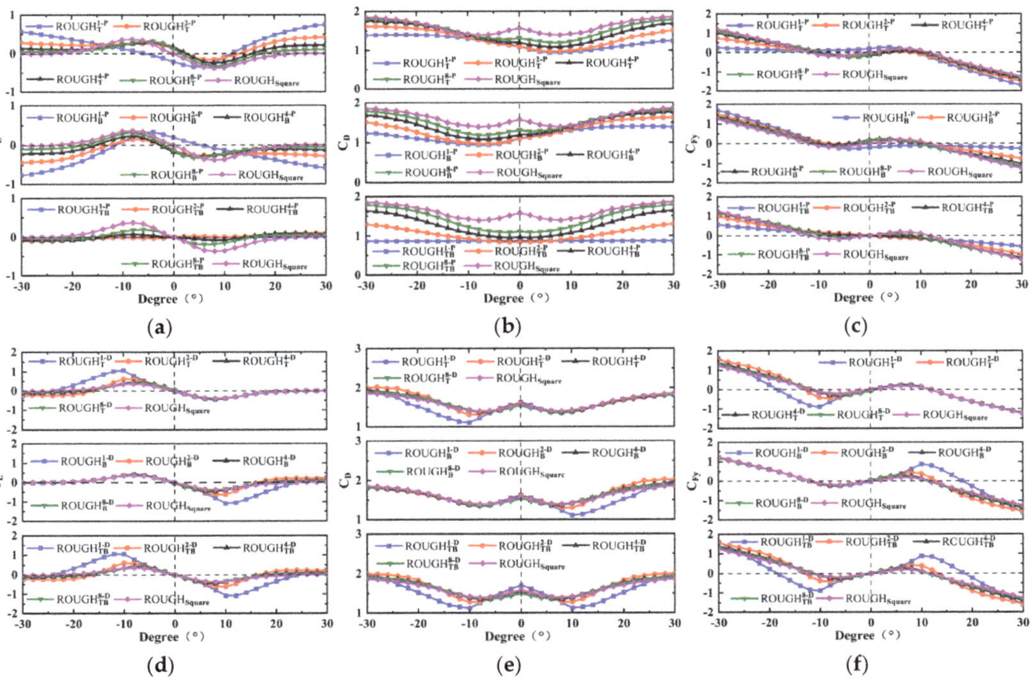

Figure 8. Numerical coefficients versus the angle of attack for protruding and depressed features on the top and/or bottom sides: (**a**) C_L, (**b**) C_D, and (**c**) C_{Fy} for the protruding feature; (**d**) C_L, (**e**) C_D, and (**f**) C_{Fy} for the depressed feature.

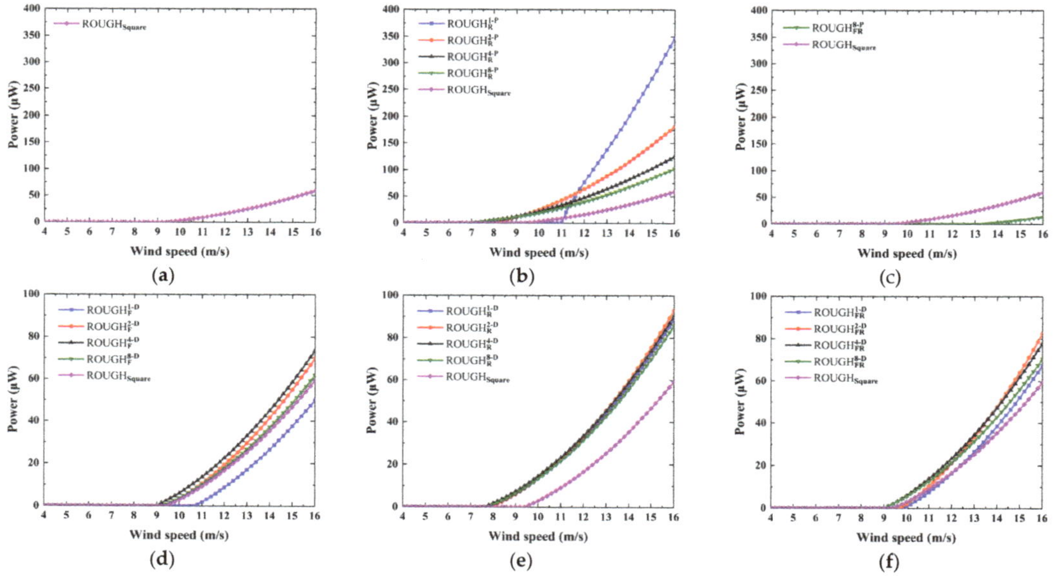

Figure 9. The numerical power versus wind speed: the protruding features on the (**a**) front side only, (**b**) rear side only, and (**c**) both front and rear side; the depressed features on the (**d**) front side only, (**e**) rear side only, and (**f**) both front and rear sides.

4. Effects of Aerodynamic Parameters on Performance of GPEH

The aerodynamic coefficient C_{Fy} is a function of the angle of attack α, and therefore of $tan(\alpha) = \dot{Y}/u$. A polynomial of $\dot{Y}/u$ can be used to approximate this function, as follows:

$$C_{Fy} = \sum_{i=0}^{N} A_i \left(\frac{\dot{Y}}{u}\right)^i, \tag{5}$$

where the symbol A_i represents the coefficients of the *ith* order $(\dot{Y}/u)$ term in the polynomial. Note that if the cross-sectional shape is symmetric in the downstream direction, the polynomial will be an odd function. The A_i of all the considered shapes is obtained using the curve fitting method, as shown in Tables A1–A9 in Appendix A, and the R-squared is configured to be no less than 0.997 to ensure that the fitted line explains most of the variability of the response data around their means. The parameters used in the model are the same as those of the prototype in Section 2, except for the aerodynamic coefficient. The wind speed step and the maximum calculation time are configured to 0.2 m/s and 100 s, respectively. The convergence condition is that the amplitude error of the displacement response between two adjacent time steps must be less than 10^{-5}, or until the calculation time reaches its maximum value. A slight displacement as an initial condition and an updated initial amplitude are also considered.

Critical wind speed and maximum power are usually used as key parameters to evaluate the performance output level of the GPEH, and the meanings of these need to be further expanded. Galloping is a typical aerodynamic instability phenomenon with self-excitation properties, which means that when the wind speed exceeds the critical wind speed, the GPEH produces a relatively high electrical output, and the electrical response level is positively correlated with the galloping amplitude or wind speed. From the perspective of application, the only purpose of structural optimization research on the

GPEH is actually to match with the spatiotemporal distribution characteristics of wind energy in a specific geographical area to achieve the best performance. The distribution characteristics can be reflected in parameters such as the average wind speed and the wind speed frequency described by probability density distribution, such as Weibull and Rayleigh distribution. In addition, the influence of material and geometric nonlinearity on the maximum output power under large deformation also needs to be considered. Based on this, in addition to the critical wind speed and maximum output power, the slope of the power versus wind speed curve should also be introduced as one of the performance evaluation parameters. The critical wind speed and maximum output power represent the working wind speed range and the ultimate performance, respectively, and the slope of the power versus wind speed curve represents the rate of the entry into the optimal performance state.

The numerical results of the investigation of power versus wind speed are shown in Figures 9 and 10. The protruding features on the front and rear sides significantly affect the galloping behavior and electrical response of the GPEH, as shown in Figure 9a–c. The introduction of the front protruding features causes the slope of C_{Fy} versus α at $\alpha = 0°$ of most of the cross-sectional shapes to be negative. The GPEHs with the above features do not experience galloping and have no electrical output, except for $ROUGH_{FR}^{1-P}$. Compared with $ROUGH_{square}$, $ROUGH_{FR}^{1-P}$ has a higher critical wind speed and lower output power. Therefore, it is necessary to avoid configuring the smooth protruding features on the front side. An interesting performance enhancement comes from the rear protruding features. All four of the considered cases can improve the performance by reducing the critical wind speed and improving the electrical response and the slope of power versus wind speed. The critical wind speed, maximum output power, and the slope k of the power versus wind speed curve of R_{square} are 9.40 m/s, 59.29 μW with 16 m/s, and $k = 1.32u - 7.78$, respectively. For the cases of $ROUGH_{R}^{1-P}$, $ROUGH_{R}^{2-P}$, $ROUGH_{R}^{4-P}$, and $ROUGH_{R}^{8-P}$, the critical wind speeds are lower than that of the $ROUGH_{square}$ by −17.0%, 14.9%, 25.5%, and 27.6%; the maximum output powers outperform it by 485.9%, 205.4%, 111.2%, 72.4%, and the slopes of the power versus wind speed curve are $k = 6.50u - 22.53$, $k = 3.46u - 18.86$, $k = 2.20u - 11.45$, and $k = 1.73u - 8.64$, respectively.

In contrast, the effects of the front and rear depressed features on the galloping behavior and electrical output are relatively weak. All the cases considered produce galloping, and the slope of power versus wind speed is almost consistent with that for the square. Due to the different critical wind speeds, the output power at the same wind speed is different. As shown in Figure 9e, the effect of the depressed feature on the C_{Fy} versus α curve is weak; consequently, the critical wind speed and slope of power versus wind speed are almost the same. The only one advantage is that those cases have a lower critical wind speed than the square, and thus have a relatively higher electrical output.

The effects of the protruding and depressed features on the top and bottom sides on the performance are shown in Figure 10. The protruding features on the top or bottom side only have a significant effect on the critical wind speed and the slope of the power versus wind speed curve, which decreases and increases with the increase in the number of semicircular protrusions, and the performance with those features is inferior to that of the square, as shown in Figure 10a,b. For the protruding features on both the top and the bottom sides, only one case of $ROUGH_{TB}^{1-P}$ can produce galloping oscillation; its critical wind speed is higher and the slope is lower than that of the square. This shows that the configuration of semicircular protruding features on the top or bottom side makes no positive contribution to the improvement of the performance of the GPEH.

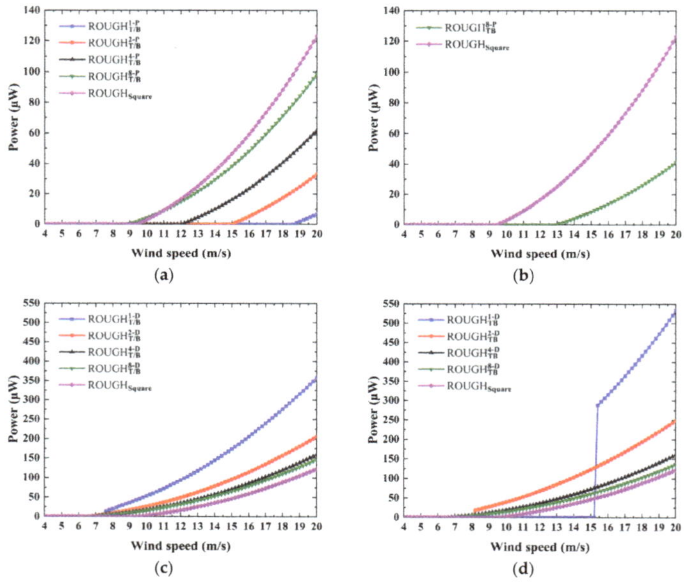

Figure 10. The numerical power versus wind speed: the protruding features on the (**a**) top or bottom side only, (**b**) both top and bottom sides; the depressed features on the (**c**) top or bottom side only, (**d**) both top and bottom sides.

Conversely, an important performance improvement comes from the depressed features, as shown in Figure 10c,d. First, the critical wind speed of all the considered cases is lower than that of the square, except for R_{TB}^{1-D}, which shows that the introduction of depressed features is an effective way to reduce the critical wind speed. Second, for cases $ROUGH_{T/B}^{1-D}$, $ROUGH_{TB}^{1-D}$, and $ROUGH_{TB}^{2-D}$, a sudden leap of the power versus wind speed curve can be found at the critical wind speed. This is because the obvious depressed features cause a larger peak value and an attack angle corresponding to $C_{Fy} = 0$, which, in turn, produces a higher galloping displacement and electrical response amplitude. For example, although the critical wind speed of $ROUGH_{TB}^{1-D}$ is 15.2 m/s, which is higher than the 9.4 m/s obtained for the square, once the wind speed exceeds the critical wind speed, the output power is 288.3 μW (15.4 m/s), which is about 5.59 times that of the square; the critical wind speed of $ROUGH_{TB}^{2-D}$ is approximately 14.9% lower, and the output power at 12 m/s is 68.1 μW and about 310.2% higher than that of the square. Finally, the asymmetric structure in the downstream direction is not considered, primarily, because it has no obvious advantages over the symmetrical structure in terms of critical wind speed and electrical response level.

Based on the aforementioned conclusions, two real-world regions representing wind-rich and wind-poor environments, such as Northern Ireland and Chongqing, China, are, respectively, considered application scenarios for the structural design of the GPEH. The theoretical critical wind speed of galloping is expressed as $u_g = \frac{4m\omega\xi}{\rho LDA_1}$, where m represents the equivalent mass. For low wind speed condition, a GPEH with a lower critical wind speed is essential. Reducing the system's equivalent mass, damping ratio, and resonant frequency can help achieve this. Consequently, the GPEH's bluff body and cantilever beam are typically fabricated using lightweight materials and flexible piezoelectric materials, respectively. Additionally, practical constraint by operational space limitation results in a finite system volume. Under identical cross-sectional dimensions, selecting a cross-sectional shape with a higher coefficient A_1 becomes preferable. Among the configurations considered in this study, those with the depressed features on the rear, top, and bottom sides exhibit higher coefficient A_1 compared to the square. The $ROUGH_{TB}^{4-D}$ has the largest coefficient A_1, with a value of 3.77, which is 1.47 times that of the square. Additionally, its slope of power versus wind speed curve is slightly larger than that of the square. For high wind speed condition, rapid transition to optimal operational states is crucial. Due to a sudden leap in the power versus wind speed curve at the critical wind speed, and a steeper slope compared to the square, $ROUGH_{T/B}^{1-D}$, $ROUGH_{TB}^{1-D}$, and $ROUGH_{TB}^{2-D}$ will have greater performance advantages in such application scenario.

5. Conclusions

In summary, research on GPEHs with diverse cross-sectional shapes has evolved from elementary shapes (e.g., square, rectangle, triangle) to complex topologies (e.g., D/W/Y/V shapes and circular or square with different rod-shaped attachments). These piecemeal early-stage studies have established a foundational knowledge through a shotgun approach. Although numerous valuable investigations have gradually expanded the understanding of the GPEH, the influence of aerodynamic coefficients primarily determined by cross-sectional shapes on performance still requires systematic and scientific consideration. Investigating methods for configuring cross-sectional shapes or identifying feature variation patterns may be an effective approach, as it helps to obtain details on how continuous feature changes affect performance. This paper provides a preliminary exploration in this research direction.

This work explored the potential effect of the protruding and depressed features on the performance of a galloping piezoelectric energy harvester. It proved that the protruding and depressed features on the bluff body can significantly change the aerodynamic characteristics, galloping behavior, and electrical performance. The evolutionary approach of the bluff body cross-sectional shape was explained, and the aerodynamic lift and drag coefficients of the forty-eight considered cross-sectional shapes were simulated using computational fluid dynamics. An experimentally verified model was used to evaluate the critical wind speed, electrical response level, and the slope of the power versus wind speed curve. There are some remarkable findings in this work, such as the fact that the protruding features should be configured on the rear side of the bluff body, rather than the front, top, and bottom sides. The depressed features should be configured on the top and bottom, rather than the front and rear sides, which is actually an effective method to reduce the critical wind speed. A symmetrical structure of the cross-sectional shape in the downstream direction should be considered as a priority, rather than an asymmetric structure. Compared with the square cross-sectional shape, there are two unconventional cases in terms of output power among all of those considered, $ROUGH_{R}^{1-P}$ and $ROUGH_{TB}^{1-D}$, and a significantly larger slope of the power versus wind speed curve was found for those two cases, respectively; thus, they represent a significant positive contribution to the optimization of high-performance harvester designs. In the future, non-semicircular protruding and depressed features, such as triangular shapes, and the height or depth of protruding and depressed features need to be considered to enhance the performance of a galloping-based piezoelectric energy harvester.

Author Contributions: Conceptualization, X.Y.; methodology, X.Y., B.X. and Z.S.; validation, B.X.; formal analysis, X.Y., B.X. and J.T.; investigation, B.X.; resources, Z.S. and J.T.; data curation, B.X.; writing—original draft preparation, X.Y. and B.X.; writing—review and editing, X.Y., B.X. and Z.S.; visualization, B.X. and X.H.; supervision, X.Y. and H.C.; project administration, X.Y. and J.T.; and funding acquisition, X.Y. All authors have read and agreed to the published version of the manuscript.

Funding: This study was supported by the National Natural Science Foundation of China [Grant number 52105574] and the Henan Science and Technology Research Plan Project [Grant numbers 242102220102].

Data Availability Statement: Data are contained within the article.

Conflicts of Interest: The authors declare no conflicts of interest.

Appendix A

Table A1. A_i and R-squared of the protruding feature on front or rear side only.

Property	$ROUGH_F^{1-P}$	$ROUGH_F^{2-P}$	$ROUGH_F^{4-P}$	$ROUGH_F^{8-P}$	$ROUGH_R^{1-P}$	$ROUGH_R^{2-P}$	$ROUGH_R^{4-P}$	$ROUGH_R^{8-P}$
A_1	−5.41	−4.09	−1.69	0.79	2.18	2.98	3.42	3.49
A_3	27	42.13	0.02	−72.1	−2.05	−36.45	−77.41	−96.59
A_5	−111	−366	−78	619	−98	58	550	791
A_7	150	1231	421	−1865	447	646	−2032	−3343
A_9		−1428	−621	−1727	−584	−3150	3698	7027
A_{11}				19,044		4055	−2612	−5820
A_{13}				−26,065				
R-square	0.99968	0.99943	0.99813	0.99982	0.99906	0.99926	0.99939	0.99967

Table A2. A_i and R-squared of the protruding feature on both front and rear sides.

Property	$ROUGH_{FR}^{1-P}$	$ROUGH_{FR}^{2-P}$	$ROUGH_{FR}^{4-P}$	$ROUGH_{FR}^{8-P}$
A_1	−0.85	−1.67	−0.35	1.81
A_3	−0.65	18.09	−10.82	−94.56
A_5	1.72	−181	−2.14	1129
A_7	−5.27	642	174.3	−7481
A_9	6.08	−776	−333	28,040
A_{11}				−55,577
A_{13}				45,099
R-square	1	0.99961	0.99905	0.99997

Table A3. A_i and R-squared of the depressed feature on front or rear side only.

Property	$ROUGH_F^{1-D}$	$ROUGH_F^{2-D}$	$ROUGH_F^{4-D}$	$ROUGH_F^{8-D}$	$ROUGH_R^{1-D}$	$ROUGH_R^{2-D}$	$ROUGH_R^{4-D}$	$ROUGH_R^{8-D}$
A_1	2.26	2.55	2.69	2.60	3.11	3.04	3.17	3.11
A_3	−64.94	−66.34	−72.21	−78.72	−84.46	−76.47	−85.77	−87.09
A_5	411	388	439	535	567	475	564	584
A_7	−1179	−1038	−1205	−1623	−1707	−1358	−1671	−1754
A_9	1248	1037	1226	1801	1878	1449	1815	1927
R-square	0.99976	0.99975	0.99918	0.99962	0.99921	0.9995	0.99978	0.99942

Table A4. A_i and R-squared of the depressed feature on both front and rear sides.

Property	$ROUGH_{FR}^{1-D}$	$ROUGH_{FR}^{2-D}$	$ROUGH_{FR}^{4-D}$	$ROUGH_{FR}^{8-D}$
A_1	2.43	2.47	2.67	2.68
A_3	−60.81	−51.44	−66.75	−74.29
A_5	365	236	391	473
A_7	−1015	−505	−1068	−1370
A_9	1053	404	1097	1464
R-square	0.99983	0.99976	0.99995	0.99976

Table A5. A_i and R-squared of the protruding feature on top or bottom side only.

Property	$ROUGH_T^{1-P}$	$ROUGH_T^{2-P}$	$ROUGH_T^{4-P}$	$ROUGH_T^{8-P}$	$ROUGH_B^{1-P}$	$ROUGH_B^{2-P}$	$ROUGH_B^{4-P}$	$ROUGH_B^{8-P}$
A_0	0.21	−0.12	−0.16	−0.13	−0.21	0.12	0.16	0.13
A_1	1.30	1.61	2.00	2.72	1.30	1.61	2.00	2.72
A_2	−5.23	7.55	13.23	12.85	5.23	−7.55	−13.23	−12.85
A_3	−86.42	−81.1	−89.98	−115.9	−86.42	−81.1	−89.98	−115.9
A_4	−51.36	−199.4	−309.7	−298.3	51.36	199.4	309.7	298.3
A_5	1203	984	996	1346	1203	984	996	1346
A_6	950	1910	3009	2927	−950	−1910	−3009	−2927
A_7	−9126	−7115	−6457	−8798	−9126	−7115	−6457	−8798
A_8	−5714	−9095	−14,557	−14,268	5714	9095	14,557	14,268
A_9	37,965	29,540	24,391	32,646	37,965	29,540	24,391	32,646
A_{10}	15,137	21,346	34,421	33,903	−15,137	−21,346	−34,421	−33,903
A_{11}	−81,107	−64,051	−49,241	−63,984	−81,107	−64,051	−49,241	−63,984
A_{12}	−14,888	−19,615	−31,626	−31,256	14,888	19,615	31,626	31,256
A_{13}	69,391	55,804	40,755	51,267	69,391	55,804	40,755	51,267
R-square	0.99977	0.99972	0.99979	0.99988	0.99977	0.99972	0.99979	0.99988

Table A6. A_i and R-squared of the protruding feature on both top and bottom sides.

Property	$ROUGH_{TB}^{1-P}$	$ROUGH_{TB}^{2-P}$	$ROUGH_{TB}^{4-P}$	$ROUGH_{TB}^{8-P}$
A_1	−0.85	−1.01	−0.06	1.86
A_3	−0.65	0.6	−25.35	−109.1
A_5	1.72	−53	130	1576
A_7	−5.27	244	−298	−14,162
A_9	6.08	−329	252	80,158
A_{11}				−274,169
A_{13}				512,202
A_{15}				−398,522
R-square	1	0.99973	0.99988	0.99995

Table A7. A_i and R-squared of the depressed feature on top or bottom side only.

Property	$ROUGH_T^{1-D}$	$ROUGH_T^{2-D}$	$ROUGH_T^{4-D}$	$ROUGH_T^{8-D}$	$ROUGH_B^{1-D}$	$ROUGH_B^{2-D}$	$ROUGH_B^{4-D}$	$ROUGH_B^{8-D}$
A_1	3.18	3.69	3.64	3.63	3.18	3.69	3.64	3.63
A_2	−18.42	−8.78	1.62	4.35	18.42	8.78	−1.62	−4.35
A_3	−27.79	−73.47	−121.69	−134.11	−27.79	−73.47	−121.69	−134.11
A_4	255.3	264.57	−10.90	−84.73	−255.3	−264.57	10.90	84.73
A_5	−2081	−325	1086	1448	−2081	−325	1086	1448
A_6	−1279.8	−2610	63	814	1279.8	2610	−63	−814
A_7	23,466	9883	−4867	−8636	23,466	9883	−4867	−8636
A_8	2300	12,194	−251	−3963	−2300	−12,194	251	3963
A_9	−117,272	−62,395	10,475	29,016	−117,272	−62,395	10,475	29,016
A_{10}	964.3	−27,528	496	9440	−964.3	27,528	−496	−9440
A_{11}	277,056	164,719	−7805	−51,445	277,056	164,719	−7805	−51,445
A_{12}	−5135	24,141	−338	−8737	5135	−24,141	338	8737
A_{13}	−251,594	−159,739	−2168	37,445	−251,594	−159,739	−2168	37,445
R-square	0.99731	0.99897	0.99987	0.99989	0.99731	0.99897	0.99987	0.99989

Table A8. A_i and R-squared of the depressed feature on both top or bottom sides.

Property	$ROUGH_{TB}^{1-D}$	$ROUGH_{TB}^{2-D}$	$ROUGH_{TB}^{4-D}$	$ROUGH_{TB}^{8-D}$
A_1	1.58	2.96	3.77	3.64
A_3	300.83	77.04	−121.40	−144.74
A_5	−9413	−5458	789	1673
A_7	115,211	83,260	1667	−10,822
A_9	−744,119	−606,911	−50,362	40,433
A_{11}	2,663,188	2,356,982	274,613	−84,710
A_{13}	−4,987,528	−4,689,992	−644,172	89,082
A_{15}	3,811,554	3,757,468	569,065	−33,869
R-square	0.99896	0.99964	0.99988	0.99994

Table A9. A_i and R-squared of the square.

Property	A_1	A_3	A_5	A_7	A_9	A_{11}	A_{13}	R-Square
R_{square}	2.56	−77.37	437	66	−9996	35,970	−39,736	0.99958

References

1. Qu, G.; Xia, H.; Liang, Q.; Liu, Y.; Ming, S.; Zhao, J.; Xia, Y.; Wu, J. Current Research Status and Future Trends of Vibration Energy Harvesters. *Micromachines* **2024**, *15*, 1109. [CrossRef] [PubMed]
2. Kang, J.G.; Kim, H.; Shin, S.; Kim, B.S. Fluid Flow to Electricity: Capturing Flow-Induced Vibrations with Micro-Electromechanical-System-Based Piezoelectric Energy Harvester. *Micromachines* **2024**, *15*, 581. [CrossRef]
3. Lian, Q.; Han, P.; Mei, N. A Review of Converter Circuits for Ambient Micro Energy Harvesting. *Micromachines* **2022**, *13*, 2222. [CrossRef] [PubMed]
4. Zhu, J.; Liu, X.; Shi, Q.; He, T.; Sun, Z.; Guo, X.; Liu, W.; Sulaiman, O.B.; Dong, B.; Lee, C. Development Trends and Perspectives of Future Sensors and Mems/Nems. *Micromachines* **2020**, *11*, 7. [CrossRef]
5. Abdelkefi, A.; Hajj, M.R.; Nayfeh, A.H. Power Harvesting from Transverse Galloping of Square Cylinder. *Nonlinear Dyn.* **2012**, *70*, 1355–1363. [CrossRef]
6. Wang, J.; Zhou, S.; Zhang, Z.; Yurchenko, D. High-Performance Piezoelectric Wind Energy Harvester with Y-Shaped Attachments. *Energy Convers. Manag.* **2019**, *181*, 645–652. [CrossRef]
7. Dai, H.L.; Abdelkefi, A.; Javed, U.; Wang, L. Modeling and Performance of Electromagnetic Energy Harvesting from Galloping Oscillations. *Smart Mater. Struct.* **2015**, *24*, 045012. [CrossRef]
8. Zhang, L.B.; Dai, H.L.; Abdelkefi, A.; Lin, S.X.; Wang, L. Theoretical Modeling, Wind Tunnel Measurements, and Realistic Environment Testing of Galloping-Based Electromagnetic Energy Harvesters. *Appl. Energy* **2019**, *254*, 113737. [CrossRef]
9. Kamilya, T.; Park, J. Highly Sensitive Self-Powered Biomedical Applications Using Triboelectric Nanogenerator. *Micromachines* **2022**, *13*, 2065. [CrossRef] [PubMed]
10. Wang, Z.L.; Jiang, T.; Xu, L. Toward the Blue Energy Dream by Triboelectric Nanogenerator Networks. *Nano Energy* **2017**, *39*, 9–23. [CrossRef]
11. Zhang, Y.L.; Wang, T.Y.; Luo, A.X.; Hu, Y.S.; Li, X.; Wang, F. Micro Electrostatic Energy Harvester with Both Broad Bandwidth and High Normalized Power Density. *Appl. Energy* **2018**, *212*, 362–371. [CrossRef]
12. Crovetto, A.; Wang, F.; Hansen, O. Modeling and Optimization of an Electrostatic Energy Harvesting Device. *J. Microelectromech. Syst.* **2014**, *23*, 1141–1155. [CrossRef]
13. Abdelkefi, A. Aeroelastic Energy Harvesting: A Review. *Int. J. Eng. Sci.* **2016**, *100*, 112–135. [CrossRef]
14. Gaidai, O.; Cao, Y.; Xing, Y.; Wang, J. Piezoelectric Energy Harvester Response Statistics. *Micromachines* **2023**, *14*, 271. [CrossRef]
15. Païdoussis, M.P.; Price, S.J.; De Langre, E. *Fluid-Structure Interactions: Cross-Flow-Induced Instabilities*; Cambridge University Press: New York, NY, USA, 2011; pp. 4–14.
16. Parkinson, G.V.; Smith, J.D. The Square Prism as an Aeroelastic Non-Linear Oscillator. *Q. J. Mech. Appl. Math.* **1964**, *17*, 225–239. [CrossRef]
17. Wang, J.L.; Geng, L.F.; Zhou, S.X.; Zhang, Z.E.; Lai, Z.H.; Yurchenko, D. Design, Modeling and Experiments of Broadband Tristable Galloping Piezoelectric Energy Harvester. *Acta Mech. Sin.* **2020**, *36*, 592–605. [CrossRef]
18. Safaei, M.; Sodano, H.A.; Anton, S.R. A Review of Energy Harvesting Using Piezoelectric Materials: State-of-the-Art a Decade Later (2008–2018). *Smart Mater. Struct.* **2019**, *28*, 113001. [CrossRef]

19. Abdelkefi, A.; Yan, Z.; Hajj, M.R. Modeling and Nonlinear Analysis of Piezoelectric Energy Harvesting from Transverse Galloping. *Smart Mater. Struct.* **2013**, *22*, 025016. [CrossRef]
20. Sirohi, J.; Mahadik, R. Piezoelectric Wind Energy Harvester for Low-Power Sensors. *J. Intell. Mater. Syst. Struct.* **2011**, *22*, 2215–2228. [CrossRef]
21. Zhao, L.Y.; Tang, L.H.; Yang, Y.W. Comparison of Modeling Methods and Parametric Study for a Piezoelectric Wind Energy Harvester. *Smart Mater. Struct.* **2013**, *22*, 125003. [CrossRef]
22. Yang, Y.w.; Zhao, L.y.; Tang, L.h. Comparative Study of Tip Cross-Sections for Efficient Galloping Energy Harvesting. *Appl. Phys. Lett.* **2013**, *102*, 064105. [CrossRef]
23. Feero, M.A.; Naguib, A.M.; Koochesfahani, M.M. Influence of Geometry on the Galloping Instability of Rectangular Cylinders in the Reynolds Number Range 1,000–10,000. *J. Fluids Struct.* **2020**, *94*, 102881. [CrossRef]
24. Yan, Z.M.; Abdelkefi, A. Nonlinear Characterization of Concurrent Energy Harvesting from Galloping and Base Excitations. *Nonlinear Dyn.* **2014**, *77*, 1171–1189. [CrossRef]
25. Wang, J.; Tang, L.; Zhao, L.; Zhang, Z. Efficiency Investigation on Energy Harvesting from Airflows in Hvac System Based on Galloping of Isosceles Triangle Sectioned Bluff Bodies. *Energy* **2019**, *172*, 1066–1078. [CrossRef]
26. Roohi, R.; Akbari, M.; Karimzadeh, A.; Amiri, M.J. Investigating the Effect of an Elliptical Bluff Body on the Behavior of a Galloping Piezoelectric Energy Harvester. *Sustainability* **2023**, *15*, 15773. [CrossRef]
27. Karimzadeh, A.; Akbari, M.; Roohi, R.; Amiri, M.J. Dynamic Behavior of Galloping Micro Energy Harvester with the Elliptical Bluff Body Using Cfd Simulation. *Sustainability* **2023**, *15*, 12187. [CrossRef]
28. Zhao, K.Y.; Zhang, Q.C.; Wang, W. Optimization of Galloping Piezoelectric Energy Harvester with V-Shaped Groove in Low Wind Speed. *Energies* **2019**, *12*, 4619. [CrossRef]
29. Zheng, J.F.; Li, Z.C.; Zhang, H. Low-Wind-Speed Galloping Wind Energy Harvester Based on a W-Shaped Bluff Body. *Energies* **2024**, *17*, 958. [CrossRef]
30. Liu, F.R.; Zou, H.X.; Zhang, W.M.; Peng, Z.K.; Meng, G. Y-Type Three-Blade Bluff Body for Wind Energy Harvesting. *Appl. Phys. Lett.* **2018**, *112*, 233903. [CrossRef]
31. Liu, F.R.; Zhang, W.M.; Peng, Z.K.; Meng, G. Fork-Shaped Bluff Body for Enhancing the Performance of Galloping-Based Wind Energy Harvester. *Energy* **2019**, *183*, 92–105. [CrossRef]
32. Ewere, F.; Wang, G.; Frendi, A. Experimental Investigation of a Bioinspired Bluff-Body Effect on Galloping Piezoelectric Energy-Harvester Performance. *AIAA J.* **2018**, *56*, 1284–1287. [CrossRef]
33. Hu, G.; Tse, K.T.; Wei, M.H.; Naseer, R.; Abdelkefi, A.; Kwok, K.C.S. Experimental Investigation on the Efficiency of Circular Cylinder-Based Wind Energy Harvester with Different Rod-Shaped Attachments. *Appl. Energy* **2018**, *226*, 682–689. [CrossRef]
34. Xing, J.; Rezaei, M.; Dai, H.; Liao, W.-H. Investigating the Effect of Surface Protrusions on Galloping Energy Harvesting. *Appl. Phys. Lett.* **2023**, *122*, 153902. [CrossRef]
35. Yang, X.K.; He, X.F.; Li, J.J.; Jiang, S.L. Modeling and Verification of Piezoelectric Wind Energy Harvesters Enhanced by Interaction between Vortex-Induced Vibration and Galloping. *Smart Mater. Struct.* **2019**, *28*, 115027. [CrossRef]
36. Yang, X.; Niu, B.; He, K.; Liu, Y.; Xie, R.; Xu, B. Parameter Effects on Performance of Piezoelectric Wind Energy Harvesters Based on the Interaction between Vortex-Induced Vibration and Galloping. *Proc. Inst. Mech. Eng. Part C J. Mech. Eng. Sci.* **2024**, *238*, 11032–11048. [CrossRef]
37. Dai, H.L.; Abdelkefi, A.; Yang, Y.; Wang, L. Orientation of Bluff Body for Designing Efficient Energy Harvesters from Vortex-Induced Vibrations. *Appl. Phys. Lett.* **2016**, *108*, 053902. [CrossRef]
38. Li, J.; He, X.; Yang, X.; Liu, Y. A Consistent Geometrically Nonlinear Model of Cantilevered Piezoelectric Vibration Energy Harvesters. *J. Sound Vib.* **2020**, *486*, 115614. [CrossRef]
39. Stanton, S.C.; Erturk, A.; Mann, B.P.; Inman, D.J. Nonlinear Piezoelectricity in Electroelastic Energy Harvesters: Modeling and Experimental Identification. *J. Appl. Phys.* **2010**, *108*, 074903. [CrossRef]
40. Laneville, A. Effects of Turbulence on Wind Induced Vibrations of Bluff Cylinders. Ph.D. Thesis, University of British Columbia, Vancouver, BC, Canada, 1973. [CrossRef]

energies

MDPI

Article

Shell-Optimized Hybrid Generator for Ocean Wave Energy Harvesting

Heng Liu [1], Dongxin Guo [2], Hengda Zhu [2], Honggui Wen [1], Jiawei Li [1] and Lingyu Wan [1,*]

1 Center on Nano-Energy Research, Institute of Science and Technology for Carbon Peak & Neutrality, Guangxi Key Laboratory for the Relativistic Astrophysics, School of Physical Science & Technology, Guangxi University, Nanning 530004, China; liuheng202503@163.com (H.L.); wenhonggui123@163.com (H.W.); lijacky413@163.com (J.L.)

2 Marine Design and Research Institute of China, Shanghai 200011, China; dongxinguo98@163.com (D.G.); zhu_h_d@163.com (H.Z.)

* Correspondence: lyw2017@gxu.edu.cn

Abstract: With the increasing global emphasis on sustainable energy, wave energy has gained recognition as a significant renewable marine resource, drawing substantial research attention. However, the efficient conversion of low-frequency, random, and low-energy wave motion into electrical power remains a considerable challenge. In this study, an advanced hybrid generator design is introduced which enhances wave energy harvesting by optimizing wave–body coupling characteristics and incorporating both a triboelectric nanogenerator (TENG) and an electromagnetic generator (EMG) within the shell. The optimized asymmetric trapezoidal shell (ATS) improves output frequency and energy harvesting efficiency in marine environments. Experimental findings under simulated water wave excitation indicate that the accelerations in the x, y, and z directions for the ATS are 1.9 $m \cdot s^{-2}$, 0.5 $m \cdot s^{-2}$, and 1.4 $m \cdot s^{-2}$, respectively, representing 1.2, 5.5, and 2.3 times those observed in the cubic shell. Under real ocean conditions, a single TENG unit embedded in the ATS achieves a maximum transferred charge of 1.54 μC, a short-circuit current of 103 μA, and an open-circuit voltage of 363 V, surpassing the cubic shell by factors of 1.21, 1.24, and 2.13, respectively. These performance metrics closely align with those obtained under six-degree-of-freedom platform oscillation (0.4 Hz, swing angle range of $\pm 6°$), exceeding the results observed in laboratory-simulated waves. Notably, the most probable output frequency of the ATS along the x-axis reaches 0.94 Hz in ocean trials, which is 1.94 times the significant wave frequency of ambient sea waves. The integrated hybrid generator efficiently captures low-quality wave energy to power water quality sensors in marine environments. This study highlights the potential of combining synergistic geometric shell design and generator integration to achieve high-performance wave energy harvesting through improved wave–body coupling.

Keywords: wave–body coupling; water wave energy harvesting; hybrid nanogenerator; asymmetric trapezoidal acrylic shell

1. Introduction

The ocean, covering the majority of the Earth's surface, sustains dynamic wave systems generated by the combined influences of wind, tides, and ocean currents [1–3]. This continuous motion represents a significant energy resource, establishing marine wave energy as a viable avenue for sustainable energy development. Wave energy possesses several advantages, including environmental sustainability, widespread availability, and

https://doi.org/10.3390/en18061502

suitability for powering offshore and remote marine infrastructures. However, its practical utilization remains challenging due to inherent properties such as low-frequency oscillations, multidirectional randomness, and spatially dispersed energy density, all of which are highly dependent on environmental conditions [4–7]. Recently, triboelectric nanogenerators (TENGs), which operate based on displacement current mechanisms, have emerged as a promising solution for harvesting high-entropy wave energy. Their advantages—such as high efficiency at low frequencies, cost-effectiveness, lightweight structure, and material versatility—address key limitations of conventional wave energy conversion technologies, attracting considerable research attention [8–12].

Various TENG and hybrid generator designs have been introduced for marine wave energy harvesting, including solid–liquid contact duct configurations [13–16], rolling sphere-based mechanisms [17–20], pendulum-type systems [21–24], biomimetic designs [25–27], multi-degree-of-freedom layered devices [28–30], and mechanically coupled systems that facilitate frequency amplification [31,32]. In marine applications, TENG units are generally enclosed within buoyant shells that harvest energy through wave-induced motion [33–36]. However, previous research has predominantly focused on optimizing TENG structures while overlooking wave–structure interactions and real ocean performance validation. The inherent dynamics of wave propagation, stochasticity, and the low-frequency nature of sea waves frequently lead to inefficient energy absorption due to the passive drift of floating TENG devices. Consequently, optimizing the shell design is essential for improving energy harvesting efficiency in both standalone TENGs and hybrid generators. Xu et al. examined the hydrodynamic responses of various shells by integrating inertial measurement units with geometric structures, determining that cubic shells exhibited superior wave absorption under laboratory wave excitation [37]. Subsequent ocean field trials (Sea State 3–4) conducted by Zhai et al. indicated that cubic shell devices exhibited significantly lower accelerations than those observed in linear motor tests or conventional wave tank simulations, suggesting suboptimal generator excitation in practical marine environments [38]. Guo et al. further introduced structural quality factors for shells and systematically analyzed the effects of geometric parameters, providing essential guidelines for buoyant generator design [39]. Through comprehensive analysis of buoyant body motion in water, combined with multidimensional dynamic simulations, Xu et al. demonstrated that wave-absorbing capacity can be effectively enhanced by increasing weight, raising the center of gravity, and modifying the shape from spherical to square [40]. Nevertheless, systematic investigations into high-performance devices that leverage synergistic shell–generator interactions remain limited.

This study introduces an asymmetric trapezoidal shell-based hybrid nanogenerator (ATS-HG) designed for broadband frequency adaptability and omnidirectional energy harvesting, achieved through a synergistic combination of geometric shell optimization and integrated triboelectric–electromagnetic dual-mode energy conversion. The device consists of four multi-layered folded contact-separation triboelectric nanogenerator (TENG) units, four sliding-mode electromagnetic generator (EMG) units incorporating magnetic flux cutting configurations, a spring-coupled inertial mass mechanism, and an asymmetric trapezoidal shell (ATS). When exposed to external stochastic excitation, the shell enhances input vibrations through an optimized wave–body coupling response. Consequently, the spring-coupled inertial mass inside the shell undergoes reciprocating motion under the influence of coordinated inertial and gravitational forces, thereby activating both TENG and EMG units with low startup thresholds and high sensitivity. An encapsulated acceleration sensor within the shell was employed to systematically investigate the acceleration characteristics of the shell and the output performance of the TENG and EMG under three conditions: simulated motion on a six-degree-of-freedom platform, laboratory-generated water waves, and real ocean wave environments. A detailed statistical analysis was conducted on the acceleration properties under real stochastic ocean wave excitation to examine the correlation between shell design and device output performance.

In six-degree-of-freedom platform tests, under oscillation conditions of 0.4 Hz and $\pm 6^{\circ}$, a single TENG unit transferred a charge of 1.6 μC, achieving a maximum peak power of 3.1 mW. The maximum open-circuit voltage and short-circuit current of the EMG were recorded as 25.0 V and 7.8 mA, respectively. Under simulated water waves in a tank, with a frequency of 0.7 Hz and a wave height of 2.3 cm, the transferred charge of a single TENG unit encapsulated within the ATS reached 1.29 μC, representing around a 10% increase compared to the results for a TENG unit encapsulated in a cubic shell. Additionally, the frequency of output exceeding 1 μC for the ATS was 2.08 times that of the cubic shell. Moreover, the most probable acceleration frequency along the x-axis for the ATS was recorded at 1.9 $m \cdot s^{-2}$, which is 1.2 times that of the cubic shell.

Under real ocean conditions, where the significant wave frequency was 0.485 Hz and the significant wave height measured 11.75 cm, the single TENG unit within the ATS-HG achieved a transferred charge of 1.54 μC, which is 2.13 times that of the TENG encapsulated in a cubic shell. When charging a 40 mF capacitor, the charging voltage within 200 s was observed to be 1.31 times that of the device with a cubic shell. Additionally, in real ocean conditions, the number of output pulses from a single TENG unit inside the ATS within 300 s was recorded as 3.29 times higher compared to that of a single TENG unit inside the cubic shell. Corresponding to these output characteristics, the most probable acceleration frequencies of the ATS along the x, y, and z axes were 0.94 Hz, 0.73 Hz, and 0.52 Hz, respectively. These values are 0.94, 0.55, and 0.11 times higher than the frequencies of the surrounding random ocean waves, indicating superior wave energy collection efficiency and high responsiveness. Ultimately, the hybrid generator integrated within the ATS effectively harvested low-quality wave energy under real ocean conditions, successfully supplying power to a water quality sensor. These results confirm the practical feasibility of synergistic geometric shell design and TENG integration for high-performance wave energy harvesting through enhanced wave–body coupling optimization. In this study, guided by the principle of wave–body coupling, we developed an ATS-HG by combining independently designed shell and generator units. The unique ATS effectively amplifies the frequency of random ocean waves, thereby enhancing overall energy conversion efficiency. A direct comparison with a conventional cubic-shell hybrid generator demonstrates this new design's superior wave energy harvesting performance.

2. Experimental Section

2.1. Fabrication of Hybrid Generator Unit

The hybrid generator unit functions as a spring pendulum with dimensions of 175 mm × 90 mm × 80 mm. The overall frame is constructed from photosensitive resin (SL resin) using 3D printing technology. The spring has a height of 35 mm, an outer diameter of 20 mm, and a wire diameter of 1 mm. The unit integrates four stacked triboelectric nanogenerators (TENGs) and two rolling-type electromagnetic generators (EMGs). Each TENG consists of ten or five vertically separated units, arranged in a serrated configuration. The TENG has an active area of 50 mm × 60 mm and is composed of a 0.08 mm thick PTFE dielectric friction layer, a 0.1 mm thick spring steel friction layer, and a 0.05 mm thick PTFE substrate film. The EMG includes four 4330-turn coils and two slender magnets positioned at the base of the pendulum. The coils measure 30 mm in outer width, 10 mm in thickness, and 0.1 mm in wire diameter, with a hollow section of 50 mm × 11 mm. The magnets have dimensions of 50 mm × 5 mm × 5 mm.

2.2. ATS-HG and the Control Group Fabrication

Six hybrid generator units are divided into two groups, each forming an integrated device. Within each group, the hybrid generator units are arranged closely along their long edges and enclosed within ATS and cubic-shell structures. The ATS consists of an upper trapezoidal section with an upper base of 57.5 cm, a lower base of 72.5 cm, and a height of 46.5 cm, along with a lower trapezoidal section featuring an upper base of 35 cm, a lower base of 44 cm, and a height of 30 cm. The total height of the ATS is 25 cm, with side angles of 10° and 25° perpendicular to the long edges of the hybrid generator units, while the remaining two side angles measure 10°. The cubic-shell housing has a total volume of 50 cm × 40 cm × 29 cm.

2.3. Measurements

A six-degree-of-freedom (6-DoF) platform (Nanjing Lingjing Automation Equipment Company, Nanjing, China, made in China) is utilized to replicate ocean wave movements, allowing for the evaluation of the ATS-HG and control groups under different frequencies and amplitudes. In a tank measuring 120 cm × 100 cm × 100 cm, 20 water pumps generate various wave environments to assess the output performance of both the ATS-HG and the control groups under simulated wave conditions. Performance testing of the ATS-HG is conducted using an electrometer (Keithley 6514, Tektronix Company in Beaverton, OR, USA, made in China) and an oscilloscope (Tektronix MDO3012, Tektronix Company in Beaverton, OR, USA, made in China), while a digital wave height gauge (CBG03) is employed to record wave height data.

3. Results and Discussion

3.1. Structural Design and Working Mechanism

In general, a floating wave energy harvester consists of two primary functional components: a buoyant shell structure and an internal hybrid generator system. As shown in Figure 1a, the energy conversion process relies on the synergistic interaction of hydrodynamic forces acting on the shell, gravitational influences, and the inertial dynamics of the internal components. These coupled interactions induce the shell to follow wave-induced motion, converting wave mechanical energy into oscillations of the shell. This mechanical energy is subsequently transformed into electrical energy through two mechanisms: (1) periodic contact-separation of the triboelectric layers within the triboelectric nanogenerator (TENG) units and (2) magnetic flux variations in the electromagnetic generator (EMG) units, generating alternating currents in external circuits. In real ocean environments, the stochastic nature of sea waves and their dynamic interactions with both the shell and internal generators play a crucial role in determining energy harvesting efficiency. To overcome these challenges, a targeted design strategy was developed, integrating optimized structural configurations of hybrid TENG architectures with hydrodynamic shell engineering (the photographs of the fabricated hybrid generator are shown in Supplementary Material Figure S9).

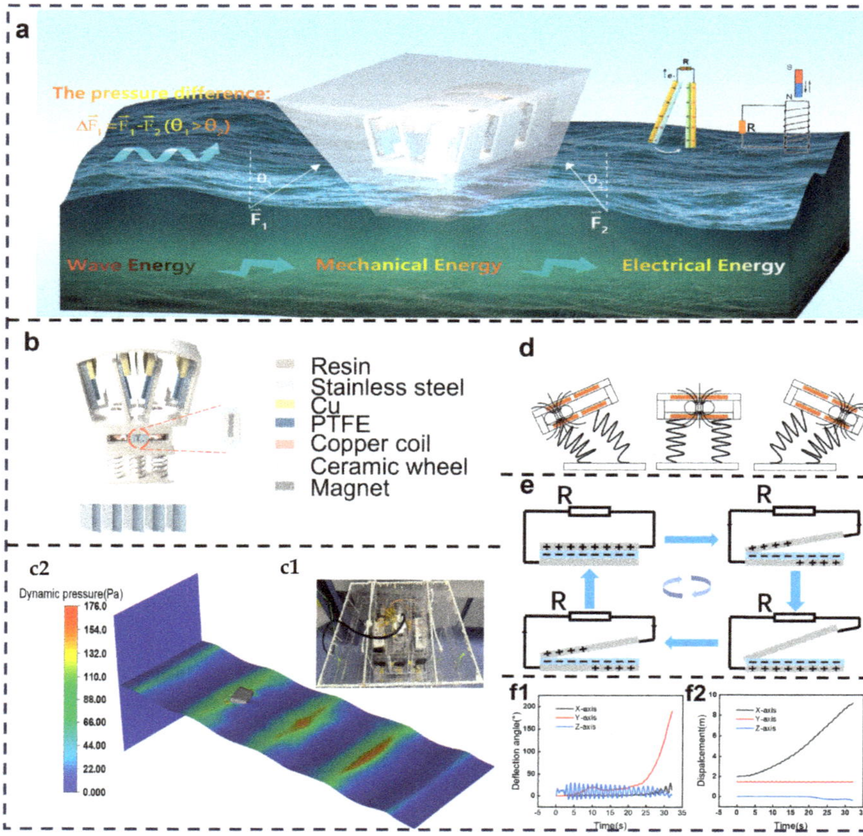

Figure 1. (**a**) Conceptual illustration of the ATS−HG for ocean energy harvesting (The arrows indicate the direction of electron movement.). (**b**) Schematic representation of the internal hybrid generator structure. (**c1**) Physical photograph of the ATS-HG. (**c2**) Motion simulation of the shell with identical parameters under finite element analysis. (**d**) Schematic of the EMG working principle. (**e**) Schematic of the TENG working principle. (**f1**) Variation in shell angle along the x, y, and z axes over time under finite element simulation. (**f2**) Variation in shell acceleration along the x, y, and z axes over time under finite element simulation.

As depicted in Figure 1b, the hybrid TENG structure primarily comprises a spring coupler and the hybrid generator body. The spring coupler consists of seven non-magnetic springs and 3D-printed supporting plates. It serves two key functions: first, it provides an elastic force to the hybrid nanogenerator body, enhancing the performance of the individual generators, lowering the operational threshold, and improving sensitivity. Second, it optimizes the coupling effect with the shell, thereby increasing the device's output frequency under low-frequency excitation. The main framework of the hybrid generator is fabricated using 3D printing and incorporates two sets of stacked TENGs, along with a rolling-type EMG. The stacked TENGs are positioned on the left and right sides of the device, while the rolling-type EMG is located at the bottom, with its working coil embedded within the device body to enhance spatial utilization. Each stacked TENG set comprises ten and five vertical contact-separation units, along with counterweight brass blocks. The working principle of the EMG is illustrated in Figure 1d. During shell oscillation, the magnet moves with the cart, while the coil remains stationary. Based on the principle of electromagnetic induction, the reciprocating motion results in variations in the magnetic flux of the coil, inducing an alternating current. The spring coupler amplifies the cart's oscillation frequency, thereby increasing the rate of magnetic flux variation while counteracting the resistance caused by the induced current. Figure 1e illustrates the working mechanism of the TENG. Utilizing electrostatic induction and triboelectric effects, charge transfer occurs when the two friction layers come into contact. The PTFE film acquires a negative charge, while the spring steel sheet becomes positively charged. As the shell moves, the brass block drives the PTFE film to separate from the spring steel sheet's surface, generating a potential difference that directs free electrons through an external circuit, producing an electric current. Upon reverse thrust, the PTFE film recontacts the spring steel sheet, generating an opposite potential difference, which results in a reverse current, forming a periodic current output.

The shell, constructed from 5 mm thick acrylic plates, features an asymmetric trapezoidal geometry, as depicted in Figure 1(c1). The inclination angles of the front and rear wave-facing surfaces are 25° and 10°, respectively, while the left and right side surfaces each have an inclination angle of 10°. Additionally, a cubic shell with the same volume was fabricated as a control, as shown in Supplementary Material Figure S1. To compare the capability of different shell designs in harvesting wave mechanical energy, finite element simulations were conducted to analyze the motion of both shells under ocean waves with a wave height of 15 cm and a frequency of 0.8 Hz, as illustrated in Figure 1(c2) and Supplementary Material Figure S1. The maximum displacement of the cubic shell's center of mass along the motion direction was determined to be 9 cm, with a maximum oscillation angle of 15.5°, as shown in Supplementary Material Figure S1. In contrast, the ATS exhibited a maximum displacement of 8.6 cm and a significantly larger maximum oscillation angle of 38°, as shown in Figure 1(f1,f2). Although the displacement of both shells was comparable, the notably greater oscillation angle of the ATS indicates its ability to induce enhanced relative motion, thereby improving the output performance of the internal hybrid TENG.

To systematically evaluate excitation levels and device output performance under different experimental conditions, an inertial measurement unit (IMU) from BEWISSENSING (BW-IMU500C) was incorporated into the shell. This IMU facilitated real-time data acquisition of acceleration along the x, y, and z axes, enabling a comprehensive analysis of device performance and its correlation with various excitation conditions across different shell hybrid TENG configurations.

3.2. The Structural Optimization

To improve the adaptability of the hybrid triboelectric nanogenerator (TENG) to oceanic wave motions and extend its energy harvesting capability across a range of wave frequencies, this study systematically examined the effect of spring coupler parameters on the performance of the hybrid TENG. Through optimization of the spring coupler design, enhanced output characteristics were achieved by improving the coupling between the spring mechanism and the hybrid generator. The influence of the presence or absence of a spring coupler on the output performance and sensitivity of the hybrid TENG was initially analyzed. In the absence of the spring coupler, a single TENG layer required a minimum angular displacement of 14° at a frequency of 0.1 Hz to facilitate effective contact separation. At this displacement, the open-circuit voltage, short-circuit current, and transferred charge of a single TENG unit were recorded as 180 V, 16 μA, and 1.1 μC, respectively. For the EMG, the minimum operating angle was determined to be 2°, with an open-circuit voltage of 3.5 V and a short-circuit current of 0.7 mA. Detailed output variations with frequency and angle are provided in Supplementary Material Figure S2. In contrast, with the integration of the spring coupler, the performance of the hybrid TENG was significantly enhanced. At 0.1 Hz, a single TENG layer required only a 4° angular displacement for effective contact separation, resulting in an open-circuit voltage, short-circuit current, and transferred charge of 420 V, 17 μA, and 1.3 μC, respectively. The EMG output also exhibited substantial improvement, with an open-circuit voltage of 8 V and a short-circuit current of 2.3 mA. Additional details regarding output variations with frequency and angle are available in Supplementary Material Figure S2. These findings indicate that the incorporation of the spring coupler considerably reduces the operational threshold of the hybrid TENG and improves sensitivity, enabling more effective adaptation to low-frequency oceanic conditions. Without the spring coupler, the hybrid TENG output increases with frequency and angle; however, beyond a certain frequency threshold, sensitivity limitations restrict further output enhancement. Excessively high frequencies may lead to insufficient contact, thereby reducing charge transfer efficiency.

To examine the coupling degree between varying spring heights and the hybrid generator body, as well as their response to wide-frequency excitation, performance comparison tests of a single TENG unit were conducted on a six-degree-of-freedom platform. Each TENG unit was equipped with a brass block to ensure adequate contact. During the experiment, the platform's swing angle was maintained at 6°, with the spring height ranging from 3.5 cm to 5 cm, and the test frequency varying from 0.1 Hz to 0.8 Hz. As illustrated in the three-dimensional color plot in Figure 2, each 3D plot is accompanied by two 2D plots on the right side, which specifically depict the output performance of the device under different test parameters. With an increase in spring height, the output frequency range of the transferred charge, open-circuit voltage, and short-circuit current progressively narrows. Higher spring heights lead to a reduced response to low-frequency excitation.

With an increase in spring height, the spring coupling undergoes greater deformation due to the gravitational force exerted by the hybrid generator body, requiring more energy for recovery. As a result, low-frequency excitation fails to effectively meet the energy demands of the spring. Notably, the frequency response range of the device is maximized when the spring height is set to 3.5 cm. Within the 0.1 Hz to 0.8 Hz frequency range, the device exhibits a balanced output performance, which increases with frequency and slightly declines after reaching saturation. This decline occurs because excessively high frequencies reduce the contact efficiency between the two friction layers of a single TENG, leading to a slight decrease in overall output. At a spring height of 3.5 cm, the peak output performance is achieved at a frequency of 0.6 Hz, with an open-circuit voltage of 580 V, a short-circuit current of 69 μA, and a transferred charge of 1.6 μC. Additionally, the energy output trend of the EMG follows a similar pattern to that of the single TENG. However, the EMG maintains stable output performance across the entire frequency range for spring heights between 3.5 cm and 5 cm due to its higher sensitivity, as it only requires movement of the device's center of gravity rather than spring recovery. The magnet-carrying cart oscillates along the track, generating a maximum open-circuit voltage of 25.0 V and a maximum short-circuit current of 7.8 mA, with detailed performance data provided in Supplementary Material Figure S3. In conclusion, a comparison of performance with and without the spring coupler demonstrated that the spring coupler effectively reduces the operational threshold of the hybrid generator. To ensure optimal electrical output performance across the entire frequency range, a spring height of 3.5 cm was selected for all device units in subsequent experiments.

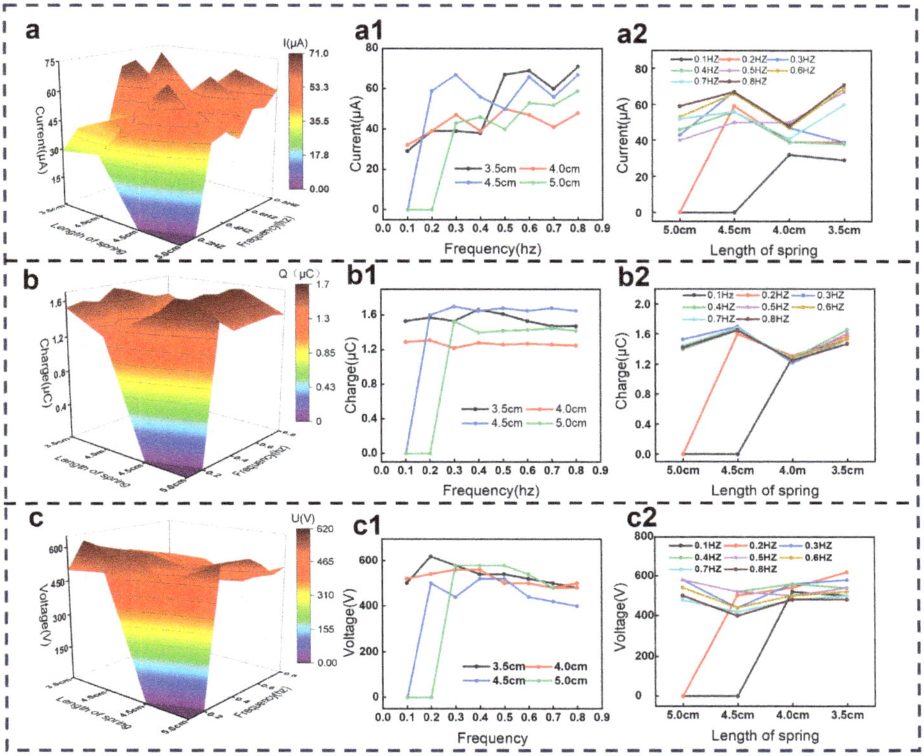

Figure 2. Output performance of a single TENG on a six-degree-of-freedom platform under varying frequencies and spring heights. (**a**) Waterfall plot showing short-circuit current variation with frequency and spring height; (**a1**) short-circuit current as a function of frequency; (**a2**) short-circuit current as a function of spring height. (**b**) Waterfall plot depicting transferred charge variation with frequency and spring height; (**b1**) transferred charge as a function of frequency; (**b2**) transferred charge as a function of spring height. (**c**) Waterfall plot illustrating open-circuit voltage variation with frequency and spring height; (**c1**) open-circuit voltage as a function of frequency; (**c2**) open-circuit voltage as a function of spring height.

3.3. Performance on 6-DoF Platform Simulating Seesaw Motions

Considering the complexity and variability of real ocean environments, the output performance of individual TENG and EMG units was further analyzed under varying input conditions, including oscillation frequency, tilt angle, impedance matching, and motion direction. All experiments were conducted using a six-degree-of-freedom platform. As shown in Figure 3a–c, when the swing angle was maintained at 6°, the short-circuit current, transferred charge, and open-circuit voltage of a single TENG unit exhibited an increasing trend with frequency, reaching a saturation point before experiencing a slight decline. At a low frequency of 0.1 Hz, the short-circuit current, transferred charge, and open-circuit voltage of the single TENG were recorded as 29 μA, 1.53 μC, and 500 V, respectively. These results indicate that the TENG unit possesses a low startup frequency adaptability, making it well-suited for low-frequency excitations prevalent in real marine environments.

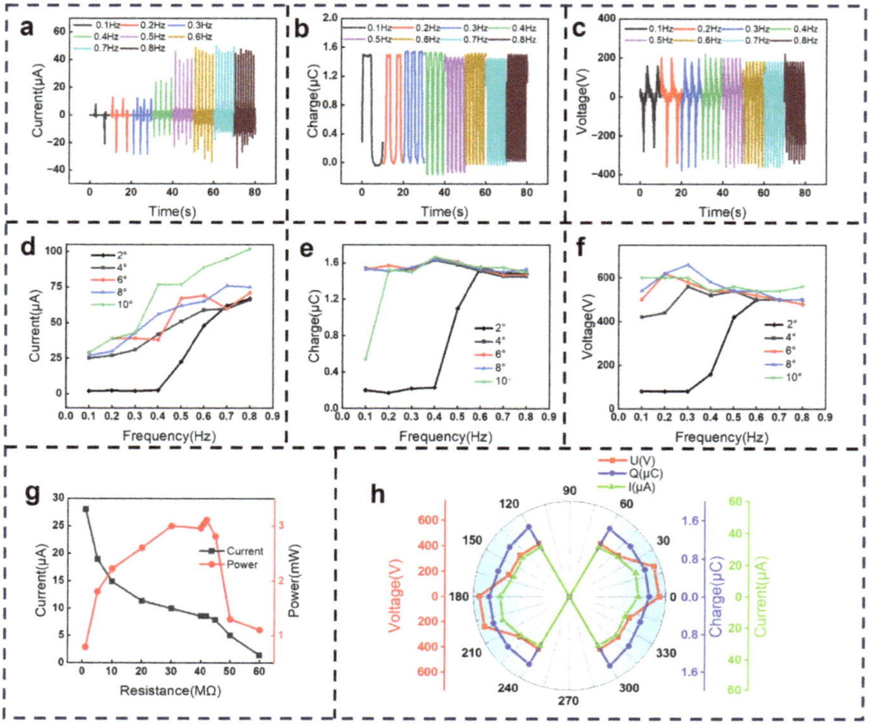

Figure 3. (**a–c**) Output performance of a single TENG unit on the six-degree-of-freedom platform at varying frequencies: (**a**) short-circuit current; (**b**) transferred charge; (**c**) open-circuit voltage. (**d–f**) Output performance of a single TENG unit on the six-degree-of-freedom platform at different frequencies and angles: (**d**) short-circuit current; (**e**) transferred charge; (**f**) open-circuit voltage. (**g**) Peak power density distribution of a single TENG unit under 0.4 Hz and 6° conditions. (**h**) Schematic representation of the horizontal effective collection range output of a single TENG unit.

Meanwhile, the short-circuit current and open-circuit voltage of the EMG unit increased with frequency, reaching 3.7 mA and 11.6 V, respectively. Additionally, as illustrated in Figure 3d–f, an increase in the swing angle resulted in a gradual decrease in the startup frequency of the single TENG. When the swing angle reached or exceeded 4°, the single TENG achieved charge saturation output of 1.54 μC under the 0.1 Hz condition. Notably, at a swing amplitude of 2°, a sharp increase was observed in the transferred charge, short-circuit current, and open-circuit voltage within the 0.4 Hz to 0.6 Hz range. Specifically, the transferred charge increased from 0.23 μC to 1.1 μC, the short-circuit current rose from 2.6 μA to 22.5 μA, and the open-circuit voltage increased from 160 V to 500 V. This phenomenon was primarily attributed to resonance between the device and the external excitation, with the resonance frequency occurring around 0.5 Hz. Furthermore, under the conditions of 0.4 Hz and a swing angle of 6°, the output power of the single TENG was analyzed across different external load resistances. As shown in Figure 3h, the maximum peak power of the single TENG was recorded at 3.1 mW when the external resistance was set to 60 MΩ.

To assess the output stability of the hybrid electromagnetic–triboelectric generator, systematic performance tests were conducted under rotational angles ranging from 0° to 360° in 20° increments using a six-degree-of-freedom (6-DoF) platform. As illustrated in Figure 3h the single TENG unit exhibited directional dependence in energy harvesting, with effective operational angular ranges of 120–240° and −300–60°. In contrast, the EMG unit displayed near-circular output profiles, confirming its capability for omnidirectional energy harvesting. The output performance of the EMG unit, presented in Supplementary Material Figure S3, further supports this observation, as the nearly circular output pattern indicates strong omnidirectional output capability. These test results suggest that while the TENG unit exhibits directional limitations in regards to energy collection, the overall device maintains efficient wave energy harvesting under full rotational motion. Consequently, the hybrid electromagnetic generator is well-suited for multi-directional wave energy collection in real marine environments.

3.4. *Power Management and Performance Comparison in Simulated Water Waves*

To assess the energy absorption efficiency and output performance of shell–device coupled systems, three hybrid generator units were encapsulated within each of two geometrically distinct acrylic shells: a cubic shell and an ATS of equal volume. In conventional laboratory testing, load output power is commonly used to evaluate device performance, typically calculated using the equations $P = I^2R$ or $P = U^2/R$ to determine the maximum instantaneous load power. However, under real ocean wave conditions, both the frequency and amplitude of the device's motion continuously vary, resulting in an absence of fixed output or optimal load power, rendering traditional load output evaluation methods inapplicable. Therefore, power generation performance was assessed by measuring the energy utilized to charge a capacitor within a fixed time period. Due to the high-voltage and low-current characteristics of the TENG output, direct rectification results in relatively low energy utilization, necessitating a power management circuit (spark-gap switch circuit) to step down the voltage and enhance the current for efficient energy extraction. In contrast, the low-voltage, high-current output of the EMG allows for direct rectification [41,42]. Both generators were connected in parallel to charge capacitors, as depicted in Figure 4a. The charging capability of the two sets of devices was tested using a six-degree-of-freedom platform, with detailed results provided in Supplementary Materials Figure S4. Under test conditions employing a 6° tilt and a frequency of 0.4 Hz, the devices encapsulated within the cubic shell charged 10 mF, 20 mF, 30 mF, 40 mF, and 50 mF capacitors to voltages of 3.81 V, 2.50 V, 1.86 V, 1.49 V, and 1.22 V, respectively, within 200 s. Under the same conditions, the other set of devices charged the capacitors to 3.43 V, 2.35 V, 1.85 V, 1.53 V, and 1.29 V, respectively. The results indicate that the charging energy of both sets of devices is comparable, primarily because the devices were fixed on the six-degree-of-freedom platform, where the external excitation directly acted on the internal device units, minimizing the influence of external shell geometry. Subsequently, a series of tests was conducted using simulated water waves generated in a wave tank. The simulated waves displayed a frequency of about 0.7 Hz and a wave height of about 2.3 cm. As shown in Figure 4b,c, charging tests were performed on 10 mF, 20 mF, 30 mF, 40 mF, and 50 mF capacitors under these simulated wave conditions. Within 200 s, the devices enclosed in the cubic shell charged the capacitors to 3.00 V, 1.94 V, 1.44 V, 1.15 V, and 1.01 V, respectively, while the devices within the ATS charged them to 4.51 V, 3.07 V, 2.32 V, 1.86 V, and 1.56 V, respectively. These values were 1.5, 1.58, 1.61, 1.62, and 1.54 times those recorded for the cubic shell, demonstrating the enhanced wave energy harvesting efficiency and coupling stability of the ATS. Further analysis of the output performance and response frequencies of the internal device units under identical wave conditions is presented in Figure 4d,e. The transferred charge of a single TENG in the ATS was measured at 1.29 μC, compared to 1.10 μC for the TENG in the cubic shell, representing an increase by a factor of 1.17. Additionally, the short-circuit current and open-circuit voltage of the TENG in the ATS were recorded at 72.46 μA and 274.49 V, respectively, which were 1.08 and 1.11 times greater than those of the cubic shell, as detailed in Supplementary Material Figure S5. The output performance of the EMG units was also evaluated under identical wave conditions. After rectification, the maximum current of the EMG unit in the ATS reached 4.45 mA, whereas in the cubic shell, it was 3.12 mA, with the former being 1.42 times the latter (detailed data are provided in Supplementary Material Figure S5). The experimental results indicate that under the consistent external excitation of the laboratory wave tank, the output waveforms of the device units remained highly stable. Additionally, the ATS exhibited superior wave absorption efficiency compared to that of the cubic shell. Enhancing the coupling between the shell and the internal device units proves to be an effective strategy for improving the overall output performance of the device.

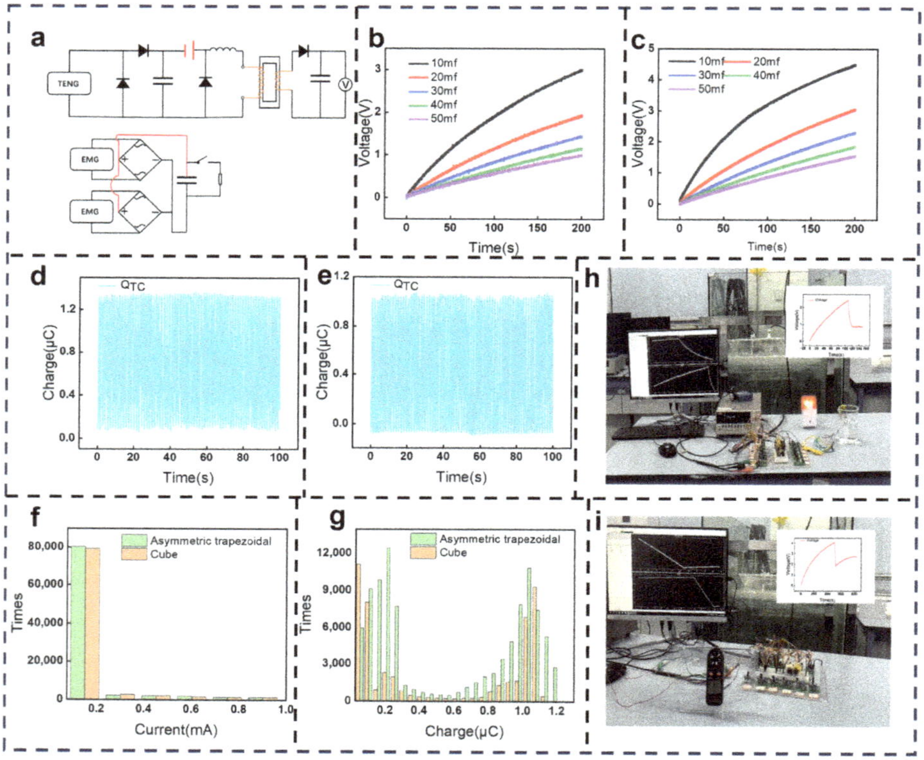

Figure 4. Performance of integrated devices with two types of shells under laboratory water tank conditions at a frequency of 0.7 Hz and a wave height of 2.3 cm. (**a**) Schematic representation of the energy management circuit for the integrated device. (**b**) Schematic illustration of the charging behavior of the integrated device with a cubic shell for different capacitances. (**c**) Schematic illustration of the charging behavior of the integrated device with an asymmetric trapezoidal enclosure for different capacitances. (**d**) Transferred charge of a single TENG under the ATS. (**e**) Transferred charge of a single TENG under the cubic enclosure. (**f**) Statistical analysis of EMG current output over 100 s. (**g**) Statistical analysis of TENG charge output over 100 s. (**h**,**i**) Operation of the water level alarm and anemometer powered by the ATS-HG: (**h**) water level alarm; (**i**) anemometer.

3.5. Acceleration Analysis and Integration of the Device in Simulated Water Waves

To further analyze the differences in wave responsiveness between the two shells, inertial measurement units (IMUs) were used to record acceleration data along the x, y, and z axes for both shells, with the results provided in Supplementary Material Figure S6. The acceleration data exhibited periodic fluctuations in both cases. Along the z-axis, the ATS recorded a peak acceleration of 2.6 $m \cdot s^{-2}$ and a trough value of 2.3 $m \cdot s^{-2}$, whereas the cubic shell exhibited a peak of 1.4 $m \cdot s^{-2}$ and a trough of 1.8 $m \cdot s^{-2}$, indicating significantly lower peak acceleration compared to that of the ATS. A similar pattern was observed along the x- and y-axes. The small difference between peak and trough values suggests relatively stable wave conditions within the wave tank. Further frequency spectrum analysis of the acceleration data along all three axes, followed by normalization and smoothing, identified the most probable frequency for both shells as 0.7 Hz, which corresponded precisely with the wave frequency of the wave tank. The complete acceleration data for both shells along the x, y, and z axes are provided in Supplementary Material Figure S6.

At this most probable frequency, the acceleration values of the ATS along the x, y, and z axes were recorded as 1.9 $m \cdot s^{-2}$, 0.5 $m \cdot s^{-2}$, and 1.4 $m \cdot s^{-2}$, respectively, which were about 1.2 times, 5.5 times, and 2.3 times those of the cubic shell. Additionally, a statistical analysis was conducted on the output performance of the transferred charge from a single TENG unit and the EMG current over a 180 s period, as shown in Figure 4f,g. For the EMG current output within the 0–0.2 mA range, the ATS recorded 80,283 occurrences, whereas the cubic shell exhibited 79,199 occurrences. Regarding the transferred charge output of a single TENG unit, the ATS recorded 34,232 instances where the transferred charge exceeded 1 μC, while the cubic shell recorded only 16,647 occurrences, making the ATS about 2.06 times more effective. The experimental results indicate that under identical wave tank excitation, the ATS exhibited significantly higher responsiveness to water waves than did the cubic shell. These findings demonstrate that optimizing shell geometry can significantly enhance the output frequency of high-sensitivity device units, thereby improving overall energy harvesting performance.

The primary goal of wave energy triboelectric nanogenerators (TENGs) is to efficiently capture wave energy and supply power to electrical devices, including IoT terminals. In this study, the energy harvesting capability of an ATS-HG was evaluated under laboratory conditions. During the experiments, the TENG unit was integrated with a spark-switch circuit, while the electromagnetic generator (EMG) unit utilized a rectifier bridge, with both generators connected in parallel. Under simulated water waves with a frequency of 0.7 Hz and a wave height of 2.3 cm, the hybrid generator successfully charged a 10 mF capacitor to 2.4 V within 107 s, enabling the operation of a water level alarm (Figure 4h, with video provided in Supplementary Material Video S1). Further testing demonstrated that the hybrid generator charged the same capacitor to 4.1 V in 500 s, allowing the operation of an anemometer for wind speed measurement (Figure 4i, with video available in Supplementary Material Video S2). These results confirm the capability of the ATS-HG to efficiently harvest wave energy for powering various electronic devices, establishing a strong foundation for future testing in real-world marine environments and potential field deployments.

3.6. Performance Comparison, Statistical Analysis, and Integration of the Device in the Real Ocean

To verify the wave absorption capability and responsiveness of the ATS under stochastic wave excitation, field trials were conducted in the coastal waters of Fangchenggang, Guangxi, China. Real-time acceleration data were recorded using an inertial measurement unit (IMU) embedded within the encapsulated shell to analyze excitation levels, as shown in Figure 5a. In the ocean, wave properties were measured using a wave height gauge, with significant wave frequency (fs) and significant wave height (hs)—defined as the average height of the highest third of the waves and the average frequency—used as parameters to assess wave motion [43]. Detailed wave property data are provided in Supplementary

Material Figure S7. Under conditions of fs = 0.485 Hz and Hs = 11.75 cm, as shown in Figure 5d, the short-circuit current of a single TENG unit encapsulated within the ATS reached 103 μA, representing a 24.1% increase compared to the 83 μA short-circuit current observed in the cubic shell. Additionally, the open-circuit voltage and transferred charge of the ATS-based TENG unit were recorded at 363 V and 1.54 μC, respectively, which were 113.5% and 21.3% higher than those measured for the cubic shell (170 V and 1.27 μC, respectively).

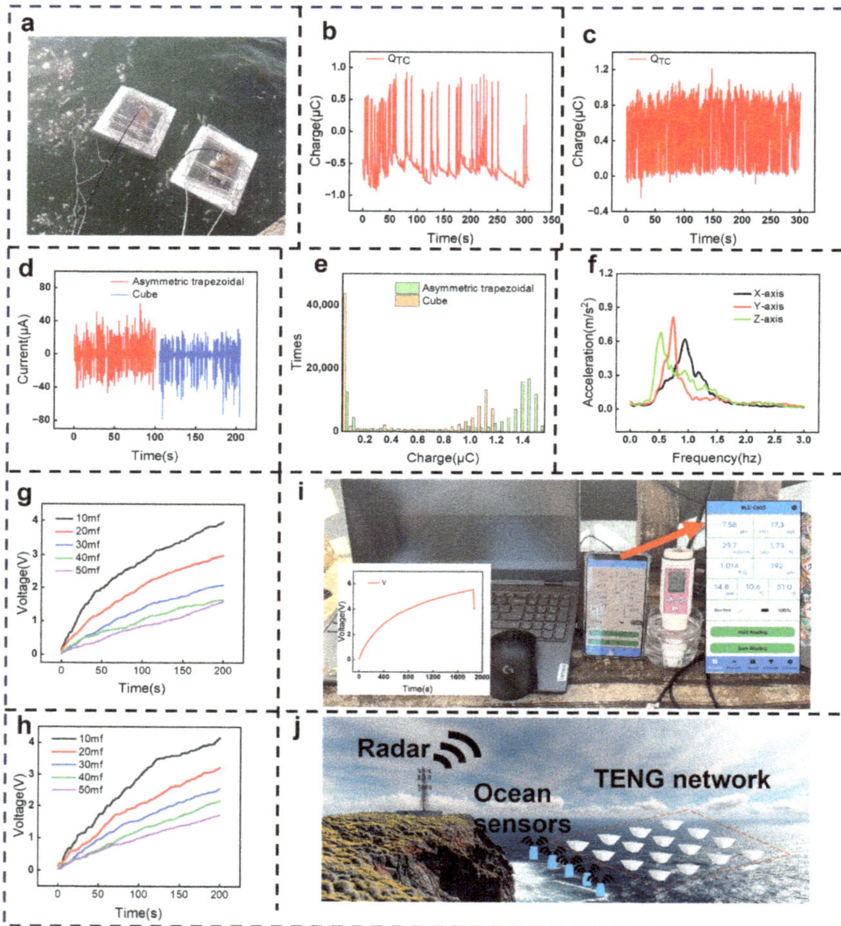

Figure 5. Under real ocean conditions, with a significant frequency of 0.485 Hz and a significant wave height of 11.75 cm: (**a**) physical image of the two types of shell-integrated devices; (**b**) charge output of a single TENG unit within the cubic shell over 300 s; (**c**) charge output of a single TENG unit within the ATS over 300 s. (**d**) Comparison of short-circuit current output from a single TENG unit under both shell types. (**e**) Statistical analysis of the charge output of a single TENG unit over 100 s for both shell types. (**f**) Acceleration distribution analysis of the ATS along the x, y, and z axes. (**g**,**h**) Charging performance of integrated devices within both shell types for different capacitor sizes in a marine test environment: (**g**) cubic shell; (**h**) ATS. (**i**) ATS-HG powering a self-sustained wireless water quality monitoring system in a real marine environment. (**j**) Schematic representation of the scenario for deploying a self-powered marine environmental wireless monitoring system.

The detailed output waveforms are provided in Supplementary Material Figure S8. Unlike the uniform and stable waves generated by the laboratory water pump, natural ocean waves consist of multiple irregular waveforms superimposed on one another, leading to unpredictable variations. Consequently, the electrical output waveforms of the hybrid generator under ocean wave excitation also exhibit irregular characteristics. The ATS demonstrated superior wave absorption capability under random wave excitation, achieving higher output performance compared to that of the cubic shell under constant excitation in the laboratory water tank. Further evaluation of the two shells' responses to random oceanic waves was conducted by measuring the transferred charge of a single TENG unit over a 300 s period. As shown in Figure 5b,c, the TENG unit encapsulated in the ATS generated 276 electrical pulse signals, with a response frequency of 0.92 Hz, whereas the TENG unit within the cubic shell produced 84 pulse signals, with a response frequency of 0.28 Hz. The response frequency of the ATS-based TENG unit was about 3.29 times higher than that of the cubic shell, indicating enhanced wave energy harvesting efficiency under stochastic wave conditions. Additionally, statistical analysis of the transfer charge output over a 100 s period is presented in Figure 5e. In the ATS, the frequency of transfer charge outputs exceeding 1 μC for the TENG unit was recorded at 71,341, whereas the corresponding frequency for the TENG unit in the cubic shell was 36,918, making the output of the former about 1.93 times higher than that of the latter. These experimental results confirm that under real oceanic random wave excitation, the ATS exhibits significantly superior wave absorption capacity and responsiveness compared to that of the cubic shell. The coupling between the ATS and the device unit enhances overall output performance, while also highlighting the limitations of laboratory-simulated ocean wave conditions. These findings emphasize the necessity for more accurate simulations that better capture the complexities of natural ocean waves in future research.

To assess the frequency amplification capability of the ATS under random wave excitation and its applicability under real ocean conditions, variations in acceleration along the x, y, and z axes inside the shell were analyzed, along with the output performance of the hybrid generator. As shown in Figure 5f, spectral analysis of the acceleration data along all three axes was conducted, followed by normalization and smoothing. The results indicated that the most probable frequencies of the ATS along the x, y, and z axes were 0.94 Hz, 0.73 Hz, and 0.52 Hz, respectively, which were 0.94 times, 0.55 times, and 0.11 times higher than the actual fs of ocean wave. These findings suggest that the ATS exhibits a strong frequency amplification effect, converting low-frequency ocean waves into higher-frequency oscillations, thereby improving coupling with the internal device and enhancing output performance. Subsequently, charging tests were conducted under ocean wave conditions of fs = 0.485 Hz and Hs = 11.75 cm using devices encapsulated in both types of shells with 10 mF, 20 mF, 30 mF, 40 mF, and 50 mF capacitors, as shown in Figure 5g,h.

The device encapsulated in the cubic shell charged the capacitors to 3.97 V, 2.99 V, 2.08 V, 1.64 V, and 1.58 V within 200 s, while the device encapsulated in the ATS achieved voltages of 4.15 V, 3.22 V, 2.54 V, 2.15 V, and 1.72 V, which were 1.05, 1.08, 1.22, 1.31, and 1.09 times higher, respectively. These results not only demonstrate the superior charging capability of the ATS but also confirm its efficient energy collection and stable coupling with the internal device unit under random wave conditions. Building upon these findings, additional application tests were conducted under identical sea conditions, leading to the successful development of a self-powered wireless water quality monitoring system. This system comprises devices encapsulated in the ATS, a data acquisition and signal transmission unit, and a receiving end. As shown in Figure 5i, after charging a 50 mF capacitor for 30 min, the voltage reached 5.54 V. The water quality detection pen was activated, and the capacitor successfully powered the device, enabling data collection and transmission to the receiving unit (video provided in Supplementary Material Video S3). In conclusion, devices encapsulated in the ATS demonstrate significant application potential in real ocean environments. As illustrated in Figure 5j, hybrid generator arrays based on these devices could be deployed near islands or across vast ocean surfaces to harness low-frequency ocean wave energy, providing power for small intelligent devices, environmental sensors, and offshore wireless communication equipment. Due to its high sensitivity to low-frequency waves, the ATS-HG is ideally suited for continuously powering distributed, low-power ocean monitoring systems, thereby reducing reliance on battery replacement or wired power sources. As a result, it holds broad application potential in oceanic Internet of things (IoT) deployments, maritime defense, underwater monitoring, and various other marine-related fields.

4. Conclusions

In summary, a hybrid nanogenerator incorporating an innovative ATS structure and integrated triboelectric–electromagnetic modules was designed and fabricated, achieving broadband frequency adaptability and omnidirectional wave energy harvesting capabilities. Finite element physical simulations were conducted to analyze the hydrodynamic performance of the ATS, demonstrating its superiority over conventional cubic geometries under controlled wave conditions. Systematic comparisons of generator outputs were performed across laboratory simulations, including six-degree-of-freedom (6-DoF) platform tests and wave tank experiments, as well as real ocean environments. Using inertial measurement units (IMUs) embedded within the shell, acceleration characteristics were systematically analyzed under both simulated laboratory water waves and real ocean wave conditions. Particular attention was given to the statistical properties of acceleration under stochastic ocean waves and the correlation between shell design and device output performance. Due to the ATS's enhanced wave collection efficiency and high responsiveness, the transferred charge of a single TENG unit encapsulated within this shell reached 1.54 μC, with a short-circuit current of 103 μA and an open-circuit voltage of 363 V, which were 1.21, 1.24, and 2.13 times higher, respectively, compared to those of the cubic shell.

Additionally, the peak charge output frequency within 300 s reached 276 pulses, which was 3.29 times higher than that of the cubic shell. The most probable acceleration frequencies along the x, y, and z axes of the ATS were 0.94 Hz, 0.73 Hz, and 0.52 Hz, respectively, corresponding to 1.94, 1.55, and 1.11 times the random wave frequencies observed in the real ocean. Under real ocean conditions, the integrated device encapsulated in the ATS successfully charged a 50 mF capacitor to 5.54 V within 30 min, enabling the operation of a Bluetooth-equipped water quality sensor and facilitating data transmission to a mobile terminal. These results highlight its potential for self-powered ocean sensing applications. This study introduces a novel approach to shell design through wave simulation and coordinated integration with energy-harvesting devices, enabling efficient wave energy conversion. The findings provide a foundation for the future optimization of high-performance wave energy harvesting systems. By first designing the shell through wave simulation based on the principle of wave–body coupling and then integrating it with the energy harvesting device, this study offers a novel approach for enhancing the performance of wave energy converters. It provides new insights into the future optimization of high-performance wave energy harvesting systems and lays a solid groundwork for large-scale, array-based applications.

Supplementary Materials: The following supporting information can be downloaded at: https://www.mdpi.com/article/10.3390/en18061502/s1, Figure S1: Photograph and simulation image of the cubic shell; Figure S2: The output performance of a single EMG and TENG with or without springs on a six-degree-of-freedom platform at different angles and frequencies; Figure S3: he output performance of a single EMG on a six-degree-of-freedom platform under varying frequencies and spring heights; Figure S4: The performance of two integrated devices with different housings on a six-degree-of-freedom platform at a frequency of 0.4 Hz and an angle of 6°; Figure S5: The performance of two integrated devices with different shells in a laboratory tank environment at a frequency of 0.7 Hz and a wave height of 2.3 cm; Figure S6: The acceleration variations of two shell-integrated devices in a laboratory tank environment at a frequency of 0.7 Hz and a wave height of 2.3 cm; Figure S7: The characteristics of real ocean waves are as follows: (a) Wave height data measured by the wave gauge over 100 seconds; Figure S8: The output performance of a single TENG in two types of shells under real ocean conditions with a significant frequency of 0.485 Hz and a significant wave height of 11.75 cm; Figure S9: Photographs of the fabricated hybrid generator; Note S1: Calculation methods of significant wave height and significant wave frequency; Video S1: The ATS-HG power for a water level alarm in the water tank; Video S2: The ATS-HG power for an anemometer for wind speed measurements in the water tank; Video S3: The ATS-HG power for a Bluetooth-equipped water quality sensor system to work in real ocean.

Author Contributions: Conceptualization, H.L. and D.G.; methodology, H.L. and H.W.; software, H.L., J.L. and H.Z.; validation, H.L., H.W. and L.W.; formal analysis, H.L. and L.W.; investigation, H.L.; data curation, H.L.; writing—original draft preparation, H.L. and L.W.; writing—review and editing, H.L. and L.W.; visualization, H.L. and L.W.; supervision, L.W.; project administration, L.W. All authors have read and agreed to the published version of the manuscript.

Funding: The research was supported by the National Key R & D Project from the Ministry of Science and Technology (2021YFA1201603) and the Natural Science Foundation of Guangxi Province (Grant No. 2021GXNSFAA075009).

Data Availability Statement: Data are contained within the article.

Acknowledgments: The research was supported by all authors.

Conflicts of Interest: The authors declare no conflicts of interest.

References

1. Zheng, C.; Shao, L.; Shi, W.; Su, Q.; Lin, G.; Li, X.; Chen, X. An assessment of global ocean wave energy resources over the last 45 a. *Acta Oceanol. Sin.* **2014**, *33*, 92–101. [CrossRef]
2. Liu, T.; Yu, J.; Yu, Y.; Zhang, X.; Zhou, B.; Yin, L. Characterization of Wave Power Resources off the Coast of Guangdong. *Processes* **2023**, *11*, 2221. [CrossRef]
3. Borthwick, A.G.L. Marine Renewable Energy Seascape. *Engineering* **2016**, *2*, 69–78. [CrossRef]
4. Mwasilu, F.; Jung, J.-W. Potential for power generation from ocean wave renewable energy source: A comprehensive review on state-of-the-art technology and future prospects. *IET Renew. Power Gener.* **2019**, *13*, 363–375. [CrossRef]
5. Kumara, K.D.R.J. On the placement of a wave manipulator suitable for energy harnessing in the Nearshore. *Cogent Eng.* **2022**, *9*, 2124636. [CrossRef]
6. Jiang, X.; Gao, D.; Hua, F.; Yang, Y.; Wang, Z. An Improved Approach to Wave Energy Resource Characterization for Sea States with Multiple Wave Systems. *J. Mar. Sci. Eng.* **2022**, *10*, 1362. [CrossRef]
7. Chen, W.; Meng, X.; Li, Y.; Gao, F. Type synthesis of parallel mechanisms capturing wave energy. *Proc. Inst. Mech. Eng. Part C-J. Mech. Eng. Sci.* **2019**, *233*, 6689–6697. [CrossRef]
8. Yan, J.; Mei, N.; Zhang, D.; Zhong, Y.; Wang, C. Review of wave power system development and research on triboelectric nano power systems. *Front. Energy Res.* **2022**, *10*, 966567. [CrossRef]
9. Salman, M.; Sorokin, V.; Aw, K. Systematic literature review of wave energy harvesting using triboelectric nanogenerator. *Renew. Sustain. Energy Rev.* **2024**, *201*, 114626. [CrossRef]
10. Hang, X.; Jiang, T.; Liu, G.; Xiao, T.; Xu, L.; Li, W.; Xi, F.; Zhang, C.; Wang, Z.L. Triboelectric Nanogenerator Networks Integrated with Power Management Module for Water Wave Energy Harvesting. *Adv. Funct. Mater.* **2019**, *29*, 1807241.
11. Wang, Z.L.; Jiang, T.; Xu, L. Toward the blue energy dream by triboelectric nanogenerator networks. *Nano Energy* **2017**, *39*, 9–23. [CrossRef]

12. Wang, Z.L. Triboelectric nanogenerators as new energy technology and self-powered sensors—Principles, problems and perspectives. *Faraday Discuss.* **2014**, *176*, 447–458. [CrossRef]
13. Zheng, Y.; Ni, Y.; Zi, Y.; Cui, H.; Li, X. Enhanced triboelectric nanogenerators in saline environments and their applications in the ocean. *Nano Energy* **2024**, *126*, 109636. [CrossRef]
14. Zhao, X.J.; Wang, H.L.; Wang, Z.L.; Wang, J. Nanocomposite Electret Layer Improved Long-Term Stable Solid-Liquid Contact Triboelectric Nanogenerator for Water Wave Energy Harvesting. *Small* **2024**, *20*, 2310023. [CrossRef]
15. Wu, M.; Guo, W.; Dong, S.; Liu, A.; Cao, Y.; Xu, Z.; Lin, C.; Zhang, J. A hybrid triboelectric nanogenerator for enhancing corrosion prevention of metal in marine environment. *npj Mater. Degrad.* **2022**, *6*, 73. [CrossRef]
16. Sun, X.; Shang, C.; Ma, H.; Li, C.; Xue, L.; Xu, Q.; Wei, Z.; Li, W.; Yalikun, Y.; Lai, Y.-C.; et al. A tube-shaped solid–liquid-interfaced triboelectric–electromagnetic hybrid nanogenerator for efficient ocean wave energy harvesting. *Nano Energy* **2022**, *100*, 107540. [CrossRef]
17. Zhao, B.; Dong, S.; Li, Z.; Zhang, B. Multi-Physics Coupling Modeling Method for the Rolling-Spherical Triboelectric Nanogenerator. *Tribology* **2020**, *40*, 680–686.
18. Liang, X.; Jiang, T.; Liu, G.; Feng, Y.; Zhang, C.; Wang, Z.L. Spherical triboelectric nanogenerator integrated with power management module for harvesting multidirectional water wave energy. *Energy Environ. Sci.* **2020**, *13*, 277–285. [CrossRef]
19. Gao, W.; Shao, J.; Sagoe-Crentsil, K.; Duan, W. Investigation on energy efficiency of rolling triboelectric nanogenerator using cylinder-cylindrical shell dynamic model. *Nano Energy* **2021**, *80*, 105583. [CrossRef]
20. Hong, H.; Chen, T.; Yang, J.; Hu, Y.; Hu, J.; Li, D.; Liu, F.; Liu, L.; Wu, H. Omnidirectional water wave energy harvesting by a spherical triboelectric nanogenerator with sliced-pizza-shaped electrodes. *Cell Rep. Phys. Sci.* **2024**, *5*, 101933. [CrossRef]
21. Zhang, C.; Yuan, W.; Zhang, B.; Yang, J.; Hu, Y.; He, L.; Zhao, X.; Li, X.; Wang, Z.L.; Wang, J. A Rotating Triboelectric Nanogenerator Driven by Bidirectional Swing for Water Wave Energy Harvesting. *Small* **2023**, *19*, 2304412. [CrossRef] [PubMed]
22. Liu, L.; Shi, Q.; Lee, C. A novel hybridized blue energy harvester aiming at all-weather IoT applications. *Nano Energy* **2020**, *76*, 105052. [CrossRef]
23. Lin, Z.; Zhang, B.; Guo, H.; Wu, Z.; Zou, H.; Yang, J.; Wang, Z.L. Super-robust and frequency-multiplied triboelectric nanogenerator for efficient harvesting water and wind energy. *Nano Energy* **2019**, *64*, 103908. [CrossRef]
24. Xu, Z.; Chen, L.; Zhang, Z.; Han, J.; Chen, P.; Hong, Z.; Jiang, T.; Wang, Z.L. Durable Roller-Based Swing-Structured Triboelectric Nanogenerator for Water Wave Energy Harvesting. *Small* **2023**, *20*, 2307288. [CrossRef]
25. Zhang, S.; Jing, Z.; Wang, X.; Zhu, M.; Yu, X.; Zhu, J.; Cheng, T.; Zhao, H.; Wang, Z.L. Soft-bionic-fishtail structured triboelectric nanogenerator driven by flow-induced vibration for low-velocity water flow energy harvesting. *Nano Res.* **2023**, *16*, 466–472. [CrossRef]
26. Jing, Z.; Zhang, J.; Wang, J.; Zhu, M.; Wang, X.; Cheng, T.; Zhu, J.; Wang, Z.L. 3D fully-enclosed triboelectric nanogenerator with bionic fish-like structure for harvesting hydrokinetic energy. *Nano Res.* **2022**, *15*, 5098–5104. [CrossRef]
27. Cao, Y.; Tao, K.; Ren, C.; Chen, Z.; Wang, Y.; Yi, H. A sea snake structure wave power generator for efficiently harvesting ocean wave energy with flexible structure. In Proceedings of the 46th Annual Conference of the IEEE-Industrial-Electronics-Society (IECON), Singapore, 18–21 October 2020; pp. 3489–3492.
28. Yar, A. High performance of multi-layered triboelectric nanogenerators for mechanical energy harvesting. *Energy* **2021**, *222*, 119949. [CrossRef]
29. Yang, X.; Huo, D.; Su, J.; He, Z. Portable Multi-Layer Capsule-Shaped Triboelectric Generator for Human Motion Energy Harvesting. *Micromachines* **2024**, *15*, 852. [CrossRef] [PubMed]
30. Li, Y.; Guo, Z.; Zhao, Z.; Gao, Y.; Yang, P.; Qiao, W.; Zhou, L.; Wang, J.; Wang, Z.L. Multi-layered triboelectric nanogenerator incorporated with self-charge excitation for efficient water wave energy harvesting. *Appl. Energy* **2023**, *336*, 120792. [CrossRef]
31. Li, S.; Chen, C.; Guo, D.; Liu, H.; Ning, H.; Liu, G.; Wan, L. Highly Sensitive Hybrid Triboelectric Nanogenerator with Ferris-Wheel-Like Structure for Ocean Wave Energy Harvesting. *Adv. Sustain. Syst.* **2024**, *8*, 2400310. [CrossRef]
32. Wen, H.; Liu, H.; Wang, X.; Liu, G.; Zhou, P.; Zhou, W.; Tuo, L.; Qu, H.; Zhai, L.; Wan, L.; et al. Enhanced hybrid generator with spring coupling effect for low-grade water wave energy harvesting. *Nano Energy* **2025**, *133*, 110488. [CrossRef]
33. Lee, K.; Lee, J.-w.; Kim, K.; Yoo, D.; Kim, D.S.; Hwang, W.; Song, I.; Sim, J.-Y. A Spherical Hybrid Triboelectric Nanogenerator for Enhanced Water Wave Energy Harvesting. *Micromachines* **2018**, *9*, 598. [CrossRef]
34. Saadatnia, Z.; Asadi, E.; Askari, H.; Zu, J.; Esmailzadeh, E. Modeling and performance analysis of duck-shaped triboelectric and electromagnetic generators for water wave energy harvesting. *Int. J. Energy Res.* **2017**, *41*, 2392–2404. [CrossRef]
35. Ryu, H.; Yoon, H.J.; Kim, S.W. Hybrid Energy Harvesters: Toward Sustainable Energy Harvesting. *Adv. Mater.* **2019**, *31*, 1802898. [CrossRef]
36. Wang, H.; Zhu, Q.; Ding, Z.; Li, Z.; Zheng, H.; Fu, J.; Diao, C.; Zhang, X.; Tian, J.; Zi, Y. A fully-packaged ship-shaped hybrid nanogenerator for blue energy harvesting toward seawater self-desalination and self-powered positioning. *Nano Energy* **2019**, *57*, 616–624. [CrossRef]

37. Xu, S.; Liu, G.; Wang, J.; Wen, H.; Cao, S.; Yao, H.; Wan, L.; Wang, Z.L. Interaction between Water Wave and Geometrical Structures of Floating Triboelectric Nanogenerators. *Adv. Energy Mater.* **2022**, *12*, 2103408. [CrossRef]
38. Zhai, L.; Wen, H.; Liu, H.; Guo, D.; Liu, G.; Qu, H.; Wan, L.; Yao, H.; Zhai, J. High-sensitivity blue-energy-shuttle and in-situ electrical behaviors in ocean. *Nano Energy* **2024**, *125*, 109546. [CrossRef]
39. Guo, D.; Chen, C.; Li, J.; Zhai, L.; Li, S.; He, S.; Feng, J.; Wan, L.; Liu, G.; Zhai, J. Structural Quality Factor of Flo-TENG under Stochastic Wave Excitation. *Adv. Sci.* **2024**, *11*, 2405165. [CrossRef]
40. Xu, S.; Zhang, J.; Su, E.; Li, C.; Tang, W.; Liu, G.; Cao, L.N.Y.; Wang, Z.L. Dynamic behavior and energy flow of floating triboelectric nanogenerators. *Appl. Energy* **2024**, *367*, 123468. [CrossRef]
41. Wang, Z.; Liu, W.; He, W.; Guo, H.; Long, L.; Xi, Y.; Wang, X.; Liu, A.; Hu, C. Ultrahigh Electricity Generation from Low-Frequency Mechanical Energy by Efficient Energy Management. *Joule* **2021**, *5*, 441–455. [CrossRef]
42. Harmon, W.; Bamgboje, D.; Guo, H.; Hu, T.; Wang, Z.L. Self-driven power management system for triboelectric nanogenerators. *Nano Energy* **2020**, *71*, 104642. [CrossRef]
43. Holthuijsen, L.H. *Waves in Oceanic and Coastal Waters*; Cambridge University Press: Cambridge, UK, 2007; p. 70, ISBN 978-0-521-86028-4.

MDPI AG
Grosspeteranlage 5
4052 Basel
Switzerland
Tel.: +41 61 683 77 34

MDPI Books Editorial Office
E-mail: books@mdpi.com
www.mdpi.com/books

www.ingramcontent.com/pod-product-compliance
Lightning Source LLC
Chambersburg PA
CBHW061510220926
51850CB00004B/220